Discipleship

Discipleship

Following Jesus in Daily Life

J. Heinrich Arnold

30TH ANNIVERSARY EDITION

Plough

Published by Plough Publishing House
Walden, New York
Robertsbridge, England
Elsmore, Australia
www.plough.com

Plough produces books, a quarterly magazine, and Plough.com to encourage people and help them put their faith into action. We believe Jesus can transform the world and that his teachings and example apply to all aspects of life. At the same time, we seek common ground with all people regardless of their creed.

Plough is the publishing house of the Bruderhof, an international Christian community. The Bruderhof is a fellowship of families and singles practicing radical discipleship in the spirit of the first church in Jerusalem (Acts 2 and 4). Members devote their entire lives to serving God, one another, and their neighbors, renouncing private property and sharing everything. To learn more about the Bruderhof's faith, history, and daily life, see Bruderhof.com.

Originally published as Discipleship: Living for Christ in the Daily Grind.

This thirtieth anniversary edition published in 2024.
ISBN: 978-1-63608-144-1
27 26 25 24 1 2 3 4 5 6

Cover linocuts by Luke Sewell.

A catalogue record for this book is available from the British Library.

Library of Congress Cataloging-in-Publication Data
Names: Arnold, J. Heinrich, 1913-1982, author.
Title: Discipleship : following Jesus in daily life / J. Heinrich Arnold.
Description: 30th anniversary edition. | Walden, New York : Plough, 2024. | Reprint of: Discipleship : living for Christ in the daily grind / J. Heinrich Arnold. Rifton, NY : Plough Pub. House, c2011. | Summary: "Sometimes provocative but always encouraging, a pastor offers sage advice for leading Christ-like lives amid the stresses of modern life"-- Provided by publisher.
Identifiers: LCCN 2024018424 (print) | LCCN 2024018425 (ebook) | ISBN 9781636081441 (paperback) | ISBN 9781636081427 (epub)
Subjects: LCSH: Christian life--Bruderhof authors. | Church Communities International--Doctrines.
Classification: LCC BV4501.3 .A758 2024 (print) | LCC BV4501.3 (ebook) | DDC 248.4/8973--dc23/eng/20240605
LC record available at https://lccn.loc.gov/2024018424
LC ebook record available at https://lccn.loc.gov/2024018425

Printed in USA

Discipleship is not a question of our own doing;
it is a matter of making room for God
so that he can live in us.

J. H. Arnold

Contents

Foreword

Discipleship is a tough book. As I began reading it, Heinrich Arnold's words touched me as a double-edged sword, calling me to choose between truth and lies, salvation and sin, selflessness and selfishness, light and darkness, God and demon. At first I wasn't sure if I wanted to be confronted in such a direct way, and I discovered some resistance in myself. I want the good news of the Gospel to be gentle, consoling, comforting, and to offer inner peace and harmony.

But Arnold reminds me that the peace of the Gospel is not the same as the peace of the world, that the consolation of the Gospel is not the same as the consolation of the world, and that the gentleness of the Gospel has little to do with the "free for all" attitude of the world. The Gospel asks for a choice, a radical choice, a choice that is not always praised, supported, and celebrated.

Still, Arnold's writing is not harsh, unbending, fanatical, or self-righteous. To the contrary, it is full of love. Tough love, but real love. It is this love that flows from the broken heart of Jesus. What makes Arnold's words so healing is that they are not based on an idea, an ideology, or a theory, but on an intimate knowledge of Jesus Christ. Jesus, the Christ, is in the center of all the suggestions, advice, and care expressed in these reflections. This is truly a Christ-centered book.

Heinrich Arnold does not speak in his own name. He speaks in the name of Jesus. He has heard clearly the words of Paul to Timothy: "Before God, and before Christ Jesus, who is to be the judge of the living and the dead, I charge you, in the name of his appearing and his kingdom: proclaim the message and, welcome or unwelcome, insist on it. Refute falsehood, correct error, give encouragement – but do all with patience and with care to instruct" (2 Tm. 4:1–2).

It is Arnold's deep rootedness in Jesus Christ that makes him a very wise, a very safe, and a very challenging guide in our spiritual journey. But there is more: his rootedness is not simply a rootedness in the Christ who lived long ago; it is a rootedness in the Christ who is present today in the life of the community of faith.

Arnold is not a pious, sentimental guide. Every word he speaks comes from his experience in community, where discipleship is lived. It is in community that we are tested and purified. It is in community that we learn what forgiveness and healing are all about. It is in community that we learn who our neighbor is. Community is the true school of love. Arnold lived community all of his life. He knew its demands and its rewards. Most of all, he knew that it is in community that we encounter the Christ of the Gospel.

I am very grateful for this book. It is a prophetic book in a time in which few people dare to speak unpopular but truly healing words.

I pray that those who read this book won't be afraid to be confronted, and I trust that the word of God that comes to them through it will bring true comfort, true consolation, true hope, and true courage.

Henri J.M. Nouwen

Introduction

Some books are easiest to describe by saying what they are not. This is not a collection of devotions or meditations, not a "feel-good" journal about walking with God, and not a guide for self-improvement or personal spiritual growth. It is, very simply, a book about discipleship – about following Christ humbly, obediently, and with an open heart. And it is written by a man whose message cannot be understood in any other way.

Johann Heinrich Arnold (1913–1982) grew up surrounded by people for whom such discipleship took shape in a dramatic way. When he was six, his parents, Eberhard and Emmy, left their upper-class home in Berlin and moved to Sannerz, a village in central Germany. There, with a small circle of friends, they set out to live in full community of goods on the basis of Acts 2 and 4 and the Sermon on the Mount. It was a time of tremendous upheaval. The same post-war restlessness that drove his father, a well-known editor, theologian, and public speaker, to this leap of faith drove thousands of others to rise up against the rigid social and religious conventions of the period and seek new ways of life. These were Heinrich's formative years, and the steady stream of young anarchists and tramps, teachers, artisans, and free-thinkers who came through the little community influenced him profoundly. All of them had abandoned the hypocrisy of a Christendom that had grown meaningless, and many felt drawn to the life of dedication and joy they found at Sannerz.

Heinrich himself felt the call to follow Christ at the age of eleven. Later, as a young man, he committed himself to life-long membership in the church community, known by then as the Bruderhof, or "place of brothers." In 1938 he was chosen as a servant of the Word, or pastor, and from 1962 until his death he served as elder for the growing Bruderhof movement.

The flock in Arnold's care was not what one could call a typical church, and he was anything but a pastor in the conventional sense of the word. He was not a charismatic personality, and he had no formal theological training. He was a true *Seelsorger* or "spiritual guide" who cared deeply for the inner and outer well-being of the communities entrusted to him. And he served his brothers and sisters in the first place as an equal who shared their daily lives in work and leisure, at communal meals, business meetings, and worship services.

The excerpts in this book were compiled and edited over several years by people who knew Arnold personally. It was no easy task to sift through the material, for there was so much to choose from, and it ranged from published articles to personal correspondence, from transcripts of worship meetings to circulars written on behalf of the congregations he served. The purpose of this selection is simply to bring to the reader the full impact of his witness.

Arnold's style is straightforward and spontaneous. He rarely spoke with notes, and when he wrote, he quickly and sometimes almost aggressively met the heart of the issue. There were those who felt he was too blunt. Yet it was precisely his simplicity that made his witness accessible to so many. His faith was not a matter of reasoned, theological terms, but something that had to be expressed in deeds: "We are tired of words; they are cheap and can be heard almost anywhere, for who will say that he is against brotherhood and love?"

Arnold was called on to address every aspect of spiritual life, personal and communal. But there is a visible thread that runs through all he wrote: Christ and his cross as the center of the universe. Again and again, Arnold insists that without meeting Christ personally – without being confronted by His message of repentance and love – there is no possibility of a living Christian faith. It mattered little, for instance, whether a problem he had to face was of a practical or an inner nature, or whether the demands of the day arose inconveniently or unannounced. Every issue was faced on the solid ground of Christ's commands. This was true not only for the internal questions of communal life but also for all matters that needed attention beyond it, such as current political events or social issues and trends.

Arnold's Christ-centeredness gave him an unusual courage to confront sin. He could not tolerate indifference to the demands of the Gospel. But just as he fought evil in others, he fought it in himself, and the fight was never against a person, but against sin. At times, this earned him the criticism of being too "emotional," but how can one who loves Christ be coolly detached when the honor of the church is at stake? "I protest against the idea that it is wrong to react with strong emotion or excitement when God is attacked, when brothers and sisters are mistreated, or when the church is harmed. I will protest my whole life long against cool soberness in the face of cruelty or anything else that destroys God's work."

It was this, too, that enabled him to call for repentance so sharply at times: "Are we ready to let Christ's Word cut deeply into us, or will we repeatedly protect and harden ourselves against it? We do not realize how often we stand in God's way. But we can ask him to cut us with his Word, even if it hurts."

With the same vigor and insistence that Arnold called for repentance, he strove for compassion and forgiveness. If anyone took seriously Jesus' injunction to forgive so that we may be forgiven, and to forgive seventy times seven, it was Arnold. People who had hurt him or broken his trust were given his undiminished trust again and again. Why? Because he believed deeply in the power of full forgiveness; because he trusted God to the depths of his being, and because this trust enabled him to overcome his fear of man.

Ironically, just as he experienced mockery and rejection because he insisted on the need for deep repentance, he was also despised because of his humility.

For even though he refused to shut an eye to sin in the church, he refused to set himself above a person who had sinned or to condone harshness and legalism toward that person. Having suffered in his own life, he identified readily with the suffering of others.

As elder of a large church community with congregations in New York, Pennsylvania, Connecticut and England, Arnold spent many hours reading, re-reading, and prayerfully considering the contents of a daily flood of letters, and his answers illustrate the humility with which he responded. When he was asked a question, he counselled, comforted, admonished, and even sharply censured, but he never criticized or belittled anyone who turned to him in trust. And though hundreds of people turned to him year after year, he always turned them onward – beyond their preoccupation with their sins or their personal holiness – to Christ.

Arnold knew well that he did not have all the answers. Often he said that he needed to think about a matter in question, or wished to consider it in prayer, or simply felt he did not know what to do about it. Asked to explain a difficult verse, an apparent contradiction, or the meaning of a mysterious passage in the Bible, he might say, "I have thought about these words a great deal, but I do not fully understand them myself. Let us leave it in trust to God. Some day it will be revealed to us" – and he would not attempt an interpretation. Though widely-read and entirely at home in the Old and New Testament, he was a man whose education was the education of the heart, whose knowledge was the knowledge of the human soul, and whose understanding of God's ways was born of his love for God, for Jesus, and for the church.

Most important, Arnold was able to listen: he listened to his brothers and sisters, he listened to friends, strangers, to critics, and most of all he listened to God: "I want to listen with my inner heart to the voice of God speaking through the brotherhood. I want to confess Jesus in our time. I want to be poor with you, spiritually poor. I want to be obedient and go where the church sends me, and to do God's will. I long for a united brotherhood, a brotherhood that gathers the scattered."

There are many aspects of Arnold's writings that one might consider at greater length – the overriding influence of his own father, Eberhard Arnold; of the German pastors Johann Christoph and Christoph Friedrich Blumhardt and their vision of the kingdom as a present reality; or of Meister Eckhart, whose mysticism is reflected in Arnold's own inclination toward the mystical. There are also Dietrich von Hildebrand and Friedrich von Gagern, whose books Arnold read and referred to often. But none of these are important in themselves. Rather, they give his message as a whole a depth and a breadth of vision that cannot be ignored. This, perhaps, is the most compelling part of Arnold's witness, for it lifts us up again and again from the pettiness of daily life and opens our eyes to perceive the greater realities we so often ignore. To use his own words:

> What a great gift it would be if we could see a little of the great vision of Jesus – if we could see beyond our small lives! Certainly our view is very limited. But we can at least ask him to call us out of our small worlds and our self-centeredness, and we can at least ask to feel the challenge of the great harvest that must be gathered – the harvest of all nations and all people, including the generations of the future.

Hela Ehrlich
Christopher Zimmerman

The Disciple

The Inner Life

When one considers the millions who call themselves Christians, the main impression one gets is that in our time the Christian religion consists almost exclusively in going to church on Sunday mornings. I know there are exceptions, but we have to be realistic: the church has very little to say to young people – they are bored by church services and preaching, and so they turn to other things. Yet people are vaguely aware that there is something wrong with their inner life. And even if they don't go to their pastor or priest about it, they do seek help, often by going to a psychiatrist. It is true that once the inner person really changes, everything else will change. But that will come about through God, not through people.

Christ taught that there should be a complete change in every person, and that this change should begin in our inner being. Peter and the apostles taught the same at Pentecost. When the people asked Peter, "What should we do?" he said, "Believe, repent, and be baptized in the name of Jesus." And when they responded, the inner change that took place carried over into the practical and economic areas of their lives. They laid everything at the feet of the apostles

Acts 2:37–38

and no longer owned anything. Everyone gave up his property voluntarily, yet since each one shared everything with the others, no one suffered need.

For our time, too, we believe in a new society like this, brought about by a change that starts in our inner being. When God enters our inner life, the change he brings will also affect our outer life. If our Christianity is a religion for Sunday morning only, it will remain shallow and empty.

What does it mean to be created in the image of God? When God breathed life into the first man, he gave every human being the possibility of experiencing the richness of heart that is in him: love, joy, humor, wrath, suffering, purity, and unity. Because all these things are familiar to us, we can see that something of God is in us – though often in a very distorted way.

The image of God is preserved most purely in children. As adults we often live very petty lives as very petty souls; our thinking centers around ourselves only and is unrelated to God. But we are created for more than this. I don't think any one of us has yet experienced to the full the richness of spirit, soul, and heart created by God for us to enjoy. Yet as his children, we are able to experience these things as no other creatures can. And he loves us so much that he sent his only Son to save us. In Paul's first letter to the Corinthians
1 Cor. 6:3 he says that the church "is to judge the angels." This

should give us an inkling of the deep meaning of our calling and of what it means that we are made in the image of God.

God created heaven, earth, and all the constellations of the universe. He also created something else, something very mysterious: the human spirit. God created this spirit and placed it in us because he wants to live in
Acts 17:24 us. The Bible says that he does not live in temples built
1 Cor. 6:19 with hands–we ourselves should be temples for him.

My father used to say to us that stupidity is the greatest sin. He did not mean simplicity of mind, but spiritual dullness: having a dead conscience and not listening in one's heart to God.

Very few people today have any idea of the riches of the human heart. Our hearts are created to experience great things; most of us have no idea of what could happen in our lives if we would overcome our stupidity and dullness. Paul says:

Eph. 3:16–19

> I pray that out of his glorious riches he may strengthen you with power through his spirit in your inner being, so that Christ may dwell in your hearts through faith. And I pray that being rooted and established in love you may have power, together with all the saints, to grasp how wide and long and

> high and deep is the love of Christ and to know this love that surpasses knowledge – that you may be filled to the measure of all the fullness of God.

If we were to grasp this one passage, we would understand the whole Gospel. We are not filled with the fullness of God and it would be arrogant to think we were. But Paul's prayer should awaken and inspire us!

Is. 55:3

God said to Israel: "Pay heed to me and listen, and your souls will live!" It is tremendously important to be able to turn to God with one's whole being and to believe that he will speak. Everything depends on our asking him to speak to us. If we hear nothing from God for a long time, it may be because there is something between us and heaven – perhaps we lack love to our brother, or we are at odds with our spouse. If this is the case, our waiting is in vain.

Of course, we cannot expect answers from God after only five minutes of silence. Think how long Jesus himself sometimes had to wait! But the more our lives belong to Christ, and the deeper our relationship with him, the more quickly he will answer us, and the more quickly he can use us for his tasks, because he knows that here is someone who is completely ready for him.

From a letter: Meister Eckhart* emphasized the importance of the listening heart, by which he meant a heart that listens to God alone. He said that God desires nothing more than a heart that detaches itself in silence from everything and turns and listens to him. This means detachment from mammon, impurity, and *schadenfreude* or malice; from lying, mistrust, and hatred; from worldly spirits and from all other spirits foreign to him.

When people are healthy and happy, or when their economic foundation is stable, they all too often become lukewarm. They may give over to God the things they feel are not healthy in them – things that bring them distress or struggle. Yet even when these things drive them to prayer, they reserve their innermost person for themselves.

The fact that we seek God at all in times of misfortune shows us that our deepest being actually hungers and thirsts for him. We should bring our fears to God; we should bring him our sickness and anguish. But this is not enough. We must give him our innermost being, our heart and soul. When we humble ourselves before him in this way and give ourselves completely over to him – when we no longer resist giving him our whole person and whole personality – then he can help

*German mystic, 1260–1328.

us, first by bringing us to bankruptcy and then by filling us with true life.

From a letter: The main thing for you should be to recognize the greatness of God and to live for him. Try to read the Bible–at least two or three chapters every day. This will open your eyes to the greatness of Jehovah, the Lord of Hosts. Then you will see how very small the search for personal happiness is.

From a letter: When the devil incites you to hate others, I advise you to find inner quiet. You know that in your deepest heart you do not want this hatred.

I can very well understand how unhappy you feel. Try, however, to become absolutely quiet inwardly, and believe that God loves you and wants to help you, even if this belief is attacked by doubts again and again. Then your fear will be slowly overcome.

If you try to fight your emotions with other emotions, you will only become more confused. You cannot straighten out your emotions, but you can trust in God: he knows your deepest heart, and he can straighten you out. Believe in him alone.

From a letter: You ask how to find inner quiet. Remember Jesus' words about prayer; they are very
Mt. 6:6 important: "Go into your room, lock the door, and

pray to your Father who is in secret, and he, who sees what is secret, will reward you." If you detach yourself from your feelings and from the excitements of your life and seek God in this detachment from self, you will find peace of heart.

From a letter: Long prayers are not always effective. Jesus even warns us against them. They are usually more pagan than Christian.

Let your prayer life be more alive! But do not force it – let it be quite free. When prayer becomes something living to you, the fire of the Spirit will flare up, and this will bring you life!

From a letter: We cannot live without a personal prayer life. We need prayer as much as we need water. All of us need times of quiet before God. Jesus clearly
Mt. 6:1–6 says that we should not make a show of our prayers; we should close the door behind us and not speak about them. Yet hidden, personal prayer is absolutely necessary and just as important as the communal prayers of the whole church.

We tend to pray only for what we want and give little thought to what God wants of us at a particular moment. I sometimes think God would answer our prayers sooner if they were directed more to doing his will, and if our hearts were moved by the good spirit to ask what God wants. Let me say it like this: God needs us every day – he needs people to carry out his will – so we should not pray for what we would like, but rather ask for the strength to do what he would have us do.

God needs people who ask for his will to be done; if no one is interested in it, he must leave his work on earth undone. But if there are people who stretch out their hands to him in longing, asking and seeking for his will to be done, then he can do something in this world. It is wrong to think that everything comes by itself, that
Mt. 6:10 nothing is expected of us. Jesus taught us to pray for God's will to be done here on earth as it is in heaven.

We must also ask for God's will to be done in our personal lives. Because the Evil One tries again and again to lead us onto the wrong path, we must turn to God daily and ask him to renew our hearts. But we should pray not only for ourselves; we should pray for the whole world – for all humanity and all nations.

From a letter: There is wrong prayer – self-willed prayer. But if the object of our prayer is in accordance with the will of Jesus, then it is right. As long as there is nothing of self-will or self-glory mixed into it, it is not wrong.

It is completely foreign to the way of Jesus to make selfish requests in his name, for instance to wish for a successful career or for a thousand dollars. When Jesus
Jn. 14:13 says, "Whatever you ask in my name, I will do," he means whatever glorifies the Father and the Son.

In our prayer life we need to listen to the spirit of God. What God wants to tell us is of greater importance than what we want to tell him. Therefore common silence shared in the faith that he wants to speak to each heart will always be meaningful for us.

We should always believe that our prayers will be answered, even if they are not answered straightaway. Daniel prayed earnestly to God for days for the forgiveness of his sins and for the forgiveness of Israel's sins. Yet he received no answer for three weeks. Then an angel appeared to him in a vision and said:

Dn. 10:12–13

> Do not be afraid, Daniel, for from the very first day that you applied your mind to understand and mortify yourself before your God, your prayers have been heard, and I have come in answer to them. But the evil angel prince of the kingdom of Persia resisted me for twenty-one days, until Michael, one of the chief princes of heaven, came to help me.

So Daniel's prayers *were* heard from the beginning, but dark powers made it difficult for the angel who answered him to break through.

Today, despite the victory of the cross, there are still dark powers at work. Our prayers, like Daniel's, may often not be answered straightaway. Yet God hears them. We should firmly believe this.

From a letter: Give everything over to Jesus. The more you give everything over to him, the more his spirit will fill you. Even the most sincere Christians go through times of inner dryness in which God wants to test them. But then he floods them with his great love. So do not despair if you feel inner dryness.

Repentance

Mk. 1:1–4

The Gospel begins with a call to repentance. Repentance means that everything must be changed. What was up must go down, and what was down must come up. Everything must be seen as God sees it. Our whole being has to be renewed; all thinking of our own has to cease. God must become the center of our thinking and feeling.

Jesus Christ came to save people, but he first called them to repent and follow him. Many Christians are attracted by his promise of salvation, but they do not want to repent fully. It is tragic that the worst enemies of Jesus are often religious people, not unbelievers. Even in Jesus' own lifetime, those who hated him most were not the soldiers who crucified him, but the very religious Pharisees and scribes, who hated his message of repentance.

When John the Baptist appeared in the wilderness of Judea, he called people to repent – to change their hearts and minds. He certainly did not flatter those

Mt. 3:7–9

who came to him. He plainly told them how far they were from God. It was not only John the Baptist who spoke of repentance. Jesus himself did, from his first teachings in the Bible to his last.

Mt. 3:2 People dislike John the Baptist's call, "Repent, for the kingdom of heaven is at hand," because they do not understand what repentance means. Repentance does not mean self-torment; nor does it mean being judged by others. It means turning away from the corruption and mammonism of fallen humankind and letting our hearts be moved by the atmosphere of the kingdom of God. Anyone who has gone through true repentance knows that it makes the heart melt like wax, that it shocks us by showing us our sinfulness. But that should not be the central experience. God must be the center of a repentant heart – God, who was revealed at the cross as love, and who alone brings reconciliation.

From a letter: All of us must undergo difficult and painful times of repentance. I plead with you to accept it, not as punishment but as grace, and I beg you not to torment yourself but to understand that Christ wants to make you free.

From a letter: Do you really know what repentance means? When a person repents he will change in such a way that everyone who meets him will feel his change of heart. In Dickens' *A Christmas Carol* it was obvious to everyone who met old Scrooge on Christmas Day that he was a different man from the evening before. I wish you such repentance.

If we trust in Jesus and the power of his death, we will find forgiveness for our sins, however evil we are or were. But we must not play with his goodness. He will judge every sin, every compromise we make with the devil. For instance, he warns us so strongly against immorality that he says we should not even glance lustfully at a woman. Let us accept his sharpness.

There are times in every person's life when God comes close. There are also such times or hours of God for each church. According to the Book of Revelation,
Rv. 2–3 Jesus spoke from heaven through John to the seven churches, telling each what it had to recognize and why it had to repent, though also encouraging it. That was surely an important hour of God for these churches.

God is infinitely good. Once he has come to a person, he may come a second, third, fourth, or even a fifth time, but he also may not. It is up to us whether we listen to him.

However strong our will to control ourselves, and however deceptive we are, God sees through everything into the depth of our hearts. Only the act of putting ourselves under his light gives us a chance for renewal. Everything is possible if we put ourselves willingly under the light of God. But if we refuse to do this, everything in our life is in danger.

Lk. 15:7–10 It is one of the most wonderful things when a person truly repents. God comes so close to a repentant soul! A heart of stone becomes a heart of flesh, and every emotion, thought, and feeling changes. A person's entire outlook changes when the gift of repentance is given to him.

We must receive a new life; we must be changed. But it is God who must change us. And he may change us in a different way from what we had wanted or imagined. Our own ideals – our own plans for inner growth or personal change – must come to an end. Every lofty position must be given up; every high human striving sacrificed. To be fit for God's new future we must be changed *by him.*

From a letter: I am sure that Jesus can give you a completely pure heart and perfect peace. At first, the closer you come to him the more you will feel judged by your sin, but in the end you will find deep joy and peace. Your seeking for God should not make life a torment. He sees that you seek him with a sincere heart. I wish you hope and courage.

2 Cor. 7:8–13 *From a letter:* Remorse opens the heart to God. The experience itself is very painful, but later you will look back on it with gratefulness as a light in your past. Repentance does not mean that you should grovel in your sin but that your heart should be softened toward God and those around you.

From a letter: I long for you to find true repentance, because it is the only hope for you in your struggle against bitterness. There is no heart so hard that God cannot touch it and melt it. I know this because there is not one of us who has not once hardened his heart against God. If only you could experience his great longing and burning love for you and for each one of us! Then you would let everything that separates you from this great love be torn away from you, however painful it might be.

God's love is like water: it seeks the lowest place. Yet we cannot make ourselves humble and lowly in our own strength. We can see ourselves for what we
1 Cor. 4:13 are – "filth and off-scourings" – only in the light of God's omnipotence, love, purity, and truth.

Once we see the darkness of sin and the horror of separation from God, we can feel something of what Jesus means by repentance. Yet repentance means more than recognizing our sin; it means turning toward the kingdom of God. It also means being ready to run around the world in order to undo all the wrong we have done – even though we know we cannot undo anything. Finally, it means giving ourselves to him who forgives and frees us from sin.

From a letter: I am grateful that you recognize your sin, but I plead with you to stop thinking about yourself, your past, and your depression. You will only become more depressed. That is not repentance. Think of your inner being as a clear pond that mirrors the sun, the stars, and the moon. If you stir up the mud at the bottom, everything will become unclear and cloudy, and the more you stir it, the cloudier it will get. Become quiet and stand firm against the devil. Then the water will clear again, and you will see in its mirror Christ's love to you and to the whole world.

Conversion

Jn. 3:1–15 In John 3 we read that we must be reborn of water and the Spirit. This cannot be understood humanly, as Nicodemus tried to understand it. Rebirth is a secret, a mystery, a miracle. But if we believe that Jesus was sent by God the Father, and if we believe in the power of the Holy Spirit, he can give us rebirth. It all depends on belief.

A decision to follow Jesus cannot be a decision to follow him for one or two years; it must be for always. Jesus said, "No one who puts his hand to the plow and looks back is fit for service in the kingdom of God." (Lk. 9:62) But if we remain faithful to him, he will wash us clean and give us unity with God and with one another, and he will grant us eternal life.

Those who want to follow Jesus must not only open their hearts to him and say, "Come into my heart and purify me"; they must also be ready to say, "I am willing to do anything you ask of me." Jesus says, "Come, all who are heavy-burdened." (Mt. 11:28) If you are willing to come to him – to let him into your heart – then you must also be willing to let him rule you and to give up your own will.

Discipleship demands that we drop everything, including everything we count as positive in ourselves. Paul was willing to lay aside the Jewish law, and we must likewise give up our good self-image, our righteousness, and our kindness, and count it all as nothing for the sake of Jesus Christ.

The radicalism of Christ's way must challenge us. He does not want to win numbers but dedicated hearts. And he does not promise security, either economic or otherwise. He seeks those who want to give themselves unreservedly to God and to their brothers, without seeking anything for themselves.

The decision to follow Christ must be a deeply personal one. But it can never mean – as someone once said to me, "Only Jesus and I remain." Discipleship must always be related to one's brothers and sisters. Therefore Jesus brings together the two commandments "Love God with all your heart, soul, and being," (Mt. 22:37–39) and "Love your neighbor as yourself." These two commandments cannot be separated. It is true that a personal religious experience must take place in one's innermost being, but it cannot be a lonely or selfish experience.

The essence of faith must become clearer to us. One may accept the teachings of the whole Bible, but without meeting Jesus himself, it will be of no value. Nor does it help to have a conviction if one has not deeply felt and experienced Jesus' character, his being, and his nature. Each soul must be personally confronted by Jesus himself.

If we grasp in our hearts the fact that Jesus died for us, it will change us completely: it will mean revolution; it will make something new out of us to the destruction of our sinful self so that we will no longer be slaves to it.

Part of the experience of true conversion is the willingness to suffer with Christ, the suffering one. I do not believe that true conversion is possible without this.

Discipleship means complete dedication. It demands everything – the whole heart, the whole mind, and the whole of life, including one's time, energy, and property – for the cause of love. Half-hearted Christianity is worse than no Christianity.

[Mt. 12:33] Jesus says, "By the fruits you will recognize the tree";
that is, by the fruits of a person's life we will recognize
whether or not he is a hypocrite. "For not everyone
[Mt. 7:21] who says 'Lord, Lord' will come into the kingdom of
God, but only those who do the will of the Father."
Doing the will of God means showing the fruits of
[Jn. 15:1–2] repentance. Jesus also says, "I am the vine, and my
Father is the vinedresser, and every branch that does
not bear fruit, he cuts away. But those who bear fruit
he purifies so that they may bear more fruit." Here we
see that we cannot simply be converted, baptized, and
"saved," and live from then on without temptation.
If we are to bear good fruit, we must repent and be
purified again and again.

[Jn. 15:4] A branch cannot bear fruit of itself–it must be
connected to the vine. In the same way, none of us
can bear fruit without a personal relationship to Jesus.
Without such a relationship we will die inwardly and
[Jn. 15:6] bear no fruit. And if we do not bear fruit, we will be
cut off the vine, thrown into the fire, and burned.
That is the great challenge: to remain on the vine–to
remain in Jesus.

Faith

Who is God, and how can we find him? One answer to this question is that something of the light of God already lies deep in each of our hearts. At times this is to be felt only in a deep longing for goodness, justice, purity, or faithfulness. But if such a longing turns to faith, we will find God.

The early Christians said that if men seek God they will find him, because he is everywhere. There is no boundary that cannot be crossed, no hindrance that
Jn. 3:1–15 cannot be overcome to find him. Think of Nicodemus, who at first would not believe that he could change in his old age. Even he found faith. We cannot excuse ourselves for not finding faith. If we knock at the door, it will open.

God comes to the heart of every person who has faith that he will come, to everyone who seeks him. But we must look for him and wait for him to come to us. If we live our lives in dullness it will not happen. We must first seek; only then will we find.

It is a miracle of faith when people find Jesus and recognize him as the Christ. We see this happen in
Jn. 4:42 John 4:42, when the Samaritans answer the woman who met Jesus at the well: "We have heard him

ourselves and know that this is indeed Christ the Savior." If only this faith were alive here and now in our church and among the many who thirst for something new!

To the Samaritans, Jesus was just a man – hungry, tired, and thirsty. No ordinary person could have seen in him the slightest trace of his identity. Who could be blamed for failing to recognize him immediately? If we met a complete stranger, we would not straightaway take him to be the Savior of the world.

Jesus' appearance was anything but that of a savior: he was a humble man; he grew up in a small town, came into conflict with religious leaders, and suffered a shameful death. Therefore it is a miracle when a person comes to believe in him. When we can say like the
Jn. 4:42 Samaritans, "This is Christ, the Savior of the world," our heart has been opened and filled with light.

From a letter: It seems that a new, green blade of living faith is beginning to grow in your heart. Guard it, and do not give in to the flesh, to self, or to any form of sin. Prove to yourself, to those around you, and to God that this is a new chapter of your life.

Faith and a good conscience are completely interwoven with one another. If we do not listen to our conscience, our faith will suffer shipwreck. And if we lose faith, we lose the possibility of having a pure and

living conscience. Therefore the Apostle says that the
Ti. 1:15 consciences of those who do not believe are not clean. It is bound to be like this, because without faith the conscience has nothing to hold on to.

I once met some people who were critical of our giving "too much" honor to Jesus. We were talking about a saying of Jesus, and one of them asked me, "Do you believe this because Jesus said it, or because it is true?" I said I believed it for both reasons: because Jesus said it and because it is true. I have always felt I should have said more; I should have been willing to be a fool and to say, "Even if I did not understand it, I would still believe it, because Jesus said it." These people were horrified that anyone could have a child-like faith in Jesus.

Anyone who has not been troubled by the scandal of Christ's suffering and his complete humiliation is ignorant of the meaning of belief in him.

Jn. 3:16–17 The Bible says, "God so loved the world that he gave his only begotten Son. He was not sent to condemn the world, but to save it." But it also says that the world will be judged because of its unbelief. We must be overwhelmed by what it means that God "so loved the world"; then we will see how terrible it is not to believe in him. We must ask God to be newly awakened to a deeper faith and belief – to a faith that meets all personal problems, all problems of communal life, and ultimately the problems of the whole world.

Lk. 22:31–33 *From a letter:* Peter told Jesus that he was willing to die for him, but he still denied him three times. No one of us can say he will have the strength to endure. Such a thing is possible only in the power of God. He alone can give us strength.

When people feel lonely and unsure of themselves, it is often because they do not believe deeply enough that God fully understands them. Paul writes that if we love
1 Cor. 13:12 fully, we will understand as we are fully understood. John's words are very important, too: God loved us
1 Jn. 4:19 before we were ever able to love him. This is what must enter our small hearts, and what we must hold on to: the love of the great Heart which understands us fully.

We live in a time when the whole world is in turmoil, and we can expect even more shaking events than we have already seen. There is only one hope, only one thing to hold on to in every situation: Jesus and his kingdom. In life and death, in joy and judgment, he remains our only Savior.

2 Tm. 3:1–9 As Paul warns us, false and dangerous teachings are widespread, also among so-called Christians. Let us therefore remain simple and childlike in our faith in the Son of God and the Son of Man, and let us build our life of brotherly love on the rock of this faith.

Why are there so many people today who cannot find faith? I think there are several reasons. Some are satisfied with what is happening; they are proud to be living in a time of great culture and civilization, and they are blind to the suffering of humankind and the whole of creation. They have lost sight of God.

Others despair. They recognize the injustice of mammon, and they suffer with those who are oppressed. But in their compassion they forget the guilt of men – the guilt we all must bear. And if they do see guilt, they see only the guilt of a certain class or nation, not that of all men. They see the creation but not the Creator. They, too, have lost sight of God.

Still others see the sin, guilt, and weakness of men, but they have no heart, no patience with the oppressed, and they do not suffer with them. Because they have lost sight of God, they do not hear the cry of all creation. They have no real faith, or they have found faith only for their own souls and not for suffering humanity.

We can find faith only if we first find God. When we have found God, we will begin to see the need of man from His viewpoint, and we will believe that He can overcome this need. Men must recognize that God loves the world even in our time. In the night of judgment that is passing over our so-called civilization, men need to hear that God still loves them and loves his creation. The message of faith is a message of love.

Doubt

Heb. 11:1, 6

From a letter: You will never be able to prove–even to yourself–that Jesus exists. Belief must be an inner experience. As long as you try to prove the object of your belief intellectually, your efforts will stand in the way of such an experience. I am not able to prove the existence of Jesus–I have nothing but my living faith. Thomas doubted that Jesus really rose from the dead;

Jn. 20:25–29

he said, "Unless I put my hand into his wounds, I will never believe." Then he saw Jesus and believed. But Jesus said, "Blessed are those who have not seen and yet believe."

To question God's love and his nearness leads to death for someone who has already given him his life. It is good to recognize evil in oneself. But we should never doubt God's great mercy, even in judgment. Doubt leads to torments that make a person feel he is living in hell. We must be led to an ever-renewed deepening of our faith.

Anyone who thinks he is too great a sinner – anyone who doubts that Jesus can help him – binds himself to the devil. He doubts the victory of the cross, and he hinders the Holy Spirit from entering his heart. This doubt must be rejected. After all, the Gospel says that Jesus carries the sin of the whole world, and that "he
Mt. 7:7–8 who seeks will find; to him who knocks the door will be opened."

Christ, the living one, died on the cross to reconcile all things to God. This reconciliation is beyond our human understanding. But we do know that it is possible for each of us, and that we are called to repent and to find it.

From a letter: The only answer to your inner torment is faith in God. This might sound theoretical, but faith *is* the only point where light can break into your life. Think of the Sermon on the Mount, where Jesus
Mt. 6:6 teaches his disciples to pray: he says that if you lock yourself in your room and pray in secret, God, who sees in secret, will reward you. Do this, and believe that God hears you. Then you can and will find God's grace. There is redemption from evil if you believe.

Lk. 12:22–26

Jn. 14:1

From a letter: Jesus warns us against worry, which is ultimately a lack of trust in the Father. Become free from worry and care; set your heart at rest and simply trust in God and in Jesus.

You write that it is always the little things that make you doubt. Do not allow this to happen. God wants to show us great things – he has been there from the beginning and with him the Word, Christ. Everything was created by him. Think in the great curves of God's creation and his eternity.

I want to encourage anyone who feels discouraged because of having made unsuccessful attempts to follow Christ. In and of ourselves we cannot follow him; we are all equally unable. But that is because our dedication to him is not complete. Only when we empty ourselves completely, when we give everything over to God, can he work. As long as we work in our own vanity, we will fail. God shows us again and again how terribly we fail and stand in his way, as a church and as individuals. Discipleship is not a question of our own doing; it is a matter of making room for God so that he can live in us.

Dogmatism

From a letter: May God give us big hearts. May we have faith in his working in all men, though without any mixture of spirits. May he give us a crystal-clear faith that includes love for all people and yet mixes with no darkness, that forgives and understands all yet does not betray one iota of the truth.

We have to embrace the whole Christ–his sharpness as well as his act of love on the cross. Christ's love
Jn. 1:29 for all men is the love of the Lamb who carries the
sin of the world. Yet he proclaims eternal damnation
Jn. 5:29–30 as necessary for the future of God's rulership of love,
unity, and justice. To change or weaken this would be to misrepresent his message.

From a letter: You state that to believe this or that is dogmatic. But such a conception is pure theology. It is the churches that are guilty–they have given millions of people the impression that certain beliefs are nothing but dogma, yet it is they who made them into dogma.

We are free of any doubt about the miracles of God. We feel completely free to believe in the miracle of Jesus' birth and the coming of God in Jesus. On the other hand, we never want to lay this as a burden on the consciences of others, and we refuse all theological fighting over the issue. We do not doubt that Jesus of Nazareth came directly from God and that he was and is one with God, but we do not want to dispute the issue on a dogmatic level. We reject all dogmatism because it kills. We hope for and believe in the Holy Spirit.

The birth of Christ happens again and again. Where two or three are together in his name, where he is accepted with the same faith as Mary's, there the living Christ will come into being. If we believe in the Holy Spirit, then the Word will become flesh in our hearts and prove itself to us as the Son of God.

This becoming flesh is a reality, but the fact that you cannot believe it makes it possible for you to participate in a church where unjust conditions remain unchanged. You attack social injustice, but you still participate in a church where the love of God does not come into the flesh and where the material world is independent of the spiritual experience. Here lies a deep separation between faith and experience. You call our beliefs dogma: in actual fact, it is any religious life that does not change life in the flesh and the economic sphere that is dogmatic and dangerous for the inner man.

We must become "narrow" in the right way – "narrow" in the sense that we live only for Christ. I do not mean at all that our lives should show more religiosity. There is no one as broadhearted as the crucified Christ, whose outstretched arms seek all men. It is a matter of decisiveness in one's heart, of living *only* for Christ. If we have this decisiveness, we will have broad hearts, though not, of course, in the worldly sense of tolerance for anything and everything.

From a letter: The main thing is that we are united in the things we find precious–love, openness, and sharing–in our struggle against coercion, in our fight against selfishness, in understanding our children, in seeking freedom from private property, and so on. It is for these things that we live together. We want to follow Jesus and none other; we want to go in his footsteps. We want God's kingdom to come to this earth.

You want a life free from the sins of society. Yet
Mt. 17:27 not even Jesus was free from the "guilt" of using unjust mammon. There is a difference between direct personal guilt and the collective guilt of fallen creation. We cannot separate ourselves from collective guilt; we would have to live alone on our own piece of land, and we would lose all contact with our fellow men. It is better to have a business relationship with a person than no relationship at all.

In what sense do you mean: "Why can't we work to reclaim the earth and help bring it back under God's power, instead of joining in the world's ways of destruction?" How shall we do what you suggest except by isolating ourselves completely from the world? Try it. Do what you want to do. You will end up with a lot of principles, but in complete loneliness and lovelessness.

From a letter: Principles themselves do not lead to lovelessness, but in my experience they often lead to disaster. I knew a man who would not use any money or the post office or a passport, and he was jailed again and again for not paying taxes. He was very firm in his principles, but he ended up losing his faith in Jesus and then all his principles too.

From a letter: Where is God in your fear of using outward religious forms? In him all was created; nothing was created without him. He gave form to everything we see in the beauty of the earth. Your longing to dispense with all forms is anti-Christian. Didn't Jesus allow himself to be baptized, and didn't he establish the Lord's Supper or Meal of Remembrance?

Formal Christianity is horrifying. But you go too far with your fears. Marriage is a form; so is the common table and the common purse. You cannot simply fear all forms, otherwise you will not be able to live a Christian life at all.

From a letter: What does it help us to share our goods or to live in community and to be of one faith, if human souls are harmed because we have too little time to love our brothers and sisters and to express this love again and again? Let us watch that we never ever become obsessed by a principle, however right and true. By itself, the "right" principle is deadly. It kills the soul. “Right” principles resulted in Gethsemane. They too easily take the place that belongs only to God, his goodness, and his grace. Our principles must be overshadowed by our love to one another and by the compassion and grace of God.

Commitment

Many people become used to a dualism in which their lives are divided into parts, and this is a great strain. We find this also among so-called religious people – perhaps especially among them. But Jesus was
Mt. 13:45–46 absolutely single-minded. He demanded that we sell all other jewels in order to buy the one pearl of great price. We should not look at one thing with one eye and try to follow him with the other. If we ponder this deeply, each of us will realize he has to confront the
Jas. 1:1–5 division in his own heart. We must give up all dividedness. We want to be of one heart and one soul both in ourselves and with our neighbor. It is a question of life and death. Unless we find singleness of heart and mind, our dividedness will tear us to pieces.

From a letter: We must be prepared to stand by our own convictions, even to suffer death for the sake of Jesus. In the Hutterite *Chronicle** there is a story about a sixteen-year-old boy, the son of a miller, who converted to the Anabaptist way of life. When he was caught and sentenced to be beheaded, a wealthy nobleman offered to take him and raise him as his own

---

* *The Chronicle of the Hutterian Brethren, Vol. I* (Vienna, 1923; English translation, Rifton, NY: 1987), a history of the Hutterites and other Anabaptists of 16th century Europe. (See pp. 64–65.)

son, if he would only recant. But the boy kept faith with God and was executed. If discipleship is really the way we want to go, we must be prepared for such sacrifice – however hard it is, and in spite of ourselves and our failures.

A promise made to God cannot be made on the strength of human faithfulness. We must depend on God's faithfulness. No one is strong enough in his own strength to endure, for instance, what the early Christian martyrs and others throughout history endured; but God is faithful. If we give ourselves to him, his angels will fight for us.

Rv. 2:4, 5

Do we still have our first love to Jesus, our readiness to give everything, even to face death for his sake? Today we have house and home, but we do not know what the future will bring. The times are very uncertain. In the course of our community's history we have had to go from one country to another. We can offer no human security. Jesus promises his disciples that they will be persecuted and that they will suffer. We can promise nothing better. Our only security is Jesus himself.

Jn. 15:20

We must not forget that Jesus taught us a way of complete love – a way that means loving even our enemies and praying for those who persecute us. As disciples of Jesus we are not promised good days only. We must be prepared for persecution. Throughout history people have been killed for their convictions. We should be thankful that we have been protected till now, but we should also be ready to suffer for our faith.

A Christian's commitment to Christ cannot be changed through circumstances. This must be quite clear. For members of my church, for instance, the larger protection of the community might be taken away at any time. But even if through persecution only one person from our communities were left, he would still be bound to his commitments.

If we love God with all our heart, soul, and being – if we live our lives for the sake of his honor and for the kingdom of God – then we can speak of him with
Ps. 28:1 assurance in our prayers as "My Lord, my rock." It does not matter if we have enemies or what those enemies say about us. We will hear the voice of God in our hearts and be faithful.

We must be faithful *to the end.* For a Christian the most dangerous time is the middle of life. At the beginning, when our faith is new, God may seem especially near to us. After a few years, however, lukewarmness often sets in. If we are dedicated, God will carry us through our middle years, though we must still be watchful. But let us not have fear. If we are true to God, nothing can separate us from his peace.

The Lower Nature

Temptation* I sometimes wonder whether we have not become too worldly in certain things. Do sports, business matters, and concern for money fill our hearts too much? These are obvious "worldly" distractions or temptations. But there is also a danger that even the gifts God gives us, such as the beauties of nature or the joys of human love, can become a substitute for the real experience of Christ.

Heb. 2:18 The Letter to the Hebrews clearly states that Jesus was tempted just like any other human being. When Jesus was tempted in the wilderness, Satan came to him and used words from scripture to tempt him. Only after Mt. 4:1–10 the third temptation did Jesus recognize him and say, "Begone, Satan."

At one time the idea of Jesus being tempted seemed blasphemous to me. Yet now I see that there is no question: he *was* tempted like any other human being. Heb. 4:15 That is what the Gospel says. In spite of this, it is clear that Jesus never sinned.

Where does temptation end and sin begin? If we are plagued or tempted by evil thoughts, that in itself is not sinning. For instance, if an impure thought comes

---

*For this section extensive use has been made of the author's book *Freedom from Sinful Thoughts* (Plough, 1997).

to us and we reject it, that is not sin. But if we buy a dirty magazine in order to indulge in sexual fantasies, that is sin.

Jas. 1:13–15

It is a question of what we do when temptation comes – what attitude we take. When Jesus was tempted by Satan, he had an answer for him each time. That is what we have to pray for: an answer to every temptation.

We will never be completely free of temptation – we should not even expect it; Jesus himself never reached this state. But we should ask God to protect us in temptation and to give us the right answer to the Tempter each time.

From a letter: I cannot say it sharply enough: if you flaunt your form or hair, or if you dress so as to tempt another person to an impure look, you commit a sin worthy of church discipline. Jesus says in the Sermon on the Mount that anyone who casts an impure look at another is guilty. But if you willingly and intentionally bring another into that temptation, you are just as guilty.

2 Cor. 10:5

Paul describes the believer's fight against evil thoughts as a victorious one in which every thought is "taken captive to obey Christ." Paul takes for granted that men have arguments and obstacles in their minds and that these must be taken captive to obey Christ. All of us must fight this battle. We should not be surprised if we are tempted; it is part of life.

The wonderful thing about Paul's words is his certainty that these thoughts can be taken captive to obey Christ. Of course, victory is not always easy. We must face the fact that a war between good and evil is being waged continually for all of humankind. It has been going on ever since man's fall, especially since Christ's death and the coming down of the Holy Spirit at Pentecost. If someone is tormented by evil thoughts, he should remember that the spiritual battle is much greater than that in his own heart. It is greater even than that of the whole church.

The Enemy is very real, and if we recognize this, we will not be lukewarm. But Christ is also very real. To find true freedom of heart, we need to experience him.

Heb. 4:15 We know from the Letter to the Hebrews that Jesus was tempted as we are; he did not sin, but he understands us in our temptation and need. Everyone–every brother and sister, and every young or old person–should know that we have a high priest, a
Heb. 5:7 king, a master who understands. Hebrews 5:7 says, "In the days of his flesh, Jesus offered up prayers and supplications with loud cries and tears to him who was able to save him." All of us are guilty of sins in the past, so we should all feel like coming before God in prayer "with loud cries and tears" and turning to him in the faith that he can save us and all those for whom we pray.

If we think evil thoughts deliberately, be they thoughts of power over other people, of impurity, of hatred, or of any other such evil, we will act on them some day. But it is very different if we are tormented by ideas, images, or thoughts we really do not want and would give anything to have a pure heart instead. With our own will it is never possible to make ourselves pure. When we are cramped up inside against something evil, it can even lead to that evil having greater power over us. But we should never forget that God sees deeper than we do. Even if we sink further and further into evil thoughts that we do not actually want, God will see we do not want them, and he will help us.

Even Jesus was tempted by the devil. But he overcame all evil by fully trusting his Father. You will be tempted too, and when you are, all that matters will be whether or not you completely trust Jesus and the power of the cross. Unless you put your trust and belief in Jesus, you will be defeated.

The feeling of being forsaken by God brings the most dreadful suffering. And for the Son of God to feel this as he died must have been such a fearful experience that we cannot grasp it. Yet in spite of it Jesus cried out, "Father, into thy hands I give my spirit." (Lk. 23:46)

Here we find the crowning of faith. Jesus' experience of godforsakenness did not take away the trust and faith he had in his and our Father; he gave his spirit into his hands.

If we want to be healed of the wounds made by Satan's tricks and arrows – by evil feelings, thoughts, or ideas – we must have the same absolute trust in Jesus as he had in God, so that even if we feel nothing yet, we give ourselves absolutely and without reserve to him with all we are and have. Ultimately, all we have is our sin. But we must lay our sin before him in trust. Then he will give us forgiveness, cleansing, and peace of heart; and these lead to a love that cannot be described.

When depression or anything other than Jesus threatens to rule our hearts, we must go to Jesus. There we will find victory and peace. I am quite sure that at the cross we can be victorious over all things that come to us in life, whatever they may be.

Sin

Many people no longer know what a good conscience is; they are burdened daily with the sins of our time. We must take care to keep our consciences pure, and we must do this from childhood on. Once we get used to living with a bad conscience, we will lose everything: our relationship with God and our love to others.

Which of us takes our struggle with sin so seriously
Heb. 5:7 that we fight with loud cries and tears? Jesus did. No one has ever fought like Jesus – no one. The devil wanted no heart more than his. And because he fought much harder than any one of us will ever have to fight, he understands our struggles. Of that we can be sure. But we do have to fight. Jesus says that those who
Mt. 16:24 want to follow him must take up their cross as he took up his. I want to challenge everyone to fight as Jesus fought – to fight until death.

Paul the Apostle spoke of himself as the greatest sinner. These were not just pious words; he really meant them. He had persecuted the early church and was responsible for many martyrs' deaths, and he knew he was an enemy of God.

At Pentecost the people in Jerusalem also saw themselves as sinners – they did not feel they were good.
Acts 2:37 They were "cut to the heart," and when the Holy Spirit came to them, they did not feel worthy of it. In fact, they saw themselves as the murderers of Christ. But because of this recognition, God could use them. If we want to be used by God, we must not talk and preach to one another about love without recognizing that each one of us, too, is actually a sinner.

Sin is not only a matter of our lower nature. We all have to fight our lower nature, but some people go further and fall into satanic sin. Satanic sin is wanting praise for oneself and wanting the glory that belongs only to God. It is the desire for power over the souls and bodies of others so as to be adored, and ultimately it is the desire to be God. It is the way of the Antichrist.

If we give ourselves to satanic sin, all the sins of our lower nature will show themselves too: impurity, mammonism, hypocrisy, envy, hatred, brutality, and finally murder.

From a letter: I thank you for your long and full account of your life and for your attempt to confess your sins fully. I have deep compassion with you when I hear about your difficult childhood. When I think what a blessed childhood I myself had, I feel ashamed; God will surely ask more of me than of you.

Your past makes me think of Jesus' words, "I came
Lk. 5:31–32 not for the healthy and the just, but for the sick and the sinners." Do not forget this; hold on to it through all hours of need and temptation.

Dear brother, we need to see and experience the whole Gospel: the exceedingly great love of Jesus to the sinner, for whom he died, but also the sharpness of his parables and his shaking words for those who do not
Mt. 8:12 repent: "There will be weeping and gnashing of teeth."

Rv. 22:12–15 Revelation 22:12–15 contains the essence of the whole Gospel: it tells of the wages paid to everyone who has done good works and of the blessing given to everyone who has purified his garments in the blood of the Lamb. But then comes a sharpness which we cannot soften: "Outside are dogs, sorcerers, and fornicators; murderers and idolaters; and all who love and practice deceit."

If we give our hearts to evil, the devil will enter us and rule us. He does this whenever we make our own gods. For the ancient Jews it was a golden calf. Today mammon – the dollar – has become a god. Therefore
Dt. 6:4–5 God's first commandment is to love him with all our
Mk. 12:30 heart, mind, and being. Of course, it is impossible to fulfill this commandment without really trusting God – without being able to believe that only good comes from him and that he always means it well with us, on the condition that we do his will.

Mk. 12:31 Jesus' second commandment, which is as important as the first, is to love our neighbor as ourselves. The devil will always whisper to us and tell us not to trust our neighbor, and if we listen to him, division, mistrust, and sin will enter our relationships. Here in America we see this especially in racism. But we see it over the whole earth: in war and in every human heart where there is hatred against another.

There is nothing you can hide from God. You might
Heb. 4:13 hide your sins from others, but ultimately they will all come to light, including your secret thoughts. Whether

an evil thought is a sin or not depends on whether you entertain it or take a stand against it. Luther said that evil thoughts come like birds flying over our heads. We cannot help that. But if we allow them to build nests on our heads, then we are responsible for them.

From a letter: I plead with you to turn away for the rest of your life from all hardness and cruelty, especially cruelty toward children and sick or weak people. What did Jesus say to his disciples when they wanted to call down fire from heaven to destroy the village that refused to take them in? He was shocked by their hard, unchildlike spirit and rebuked them: "You do
Lk. 9:55–56 not know to what spirit you belong. The Son of Man did not come to destroy men's lives, but to save them." Think always of Jesus; then your heart will change.

From a letter: I do not understand why you came to the church and lied. When Ananias and Sapphira came to join the church at Jerusalem but held back their money dishonestly, Peter asked them, "How did you
Acts 5:4 contrive such an act in your hearts? You have lied not to men but to God." He also told them they could have stayed away from the church and kept what they had for themselves.

Why do you come to join us if at the same time you burden your conscience by lying to God and to us?

You will have to give an account for this. Man's destiny
Heb. 9:27 is to die; after that he must be judged by God. If you do not want to face judgment now, you will have to face it later. We will not force you. Hebrews 10:26–27
Heb. 10:26–27 says, "If we remain willingly in our sin after we have recognized the truth, there will be no sacrifice for us anymore, but only the expectation of terrible judgment and the wrath of fire."

Heb. 12:15 Hebrews 12:15 says that no one should forfeit the hour of God's grace. You are free to continue playing with God, but then we can have nothing to do with you, and you will have to answer to God alone. There is still a chance for you to turn around!

Rom. 8:1–2 "There is no condemnation for those who are united with Jesus Christ, because in him the life-giving law of the Spirit has set you free from the law of sin and death." This is such a joyful thought – all sin is overcome. But if we look at our own experience we see that it is not overcome everywhere, and the reason is simply that we are not living in Christ Jesus but in our old nature. It is an illusion to think that we do not have this lower nature. We have come into the world with it, and we ourselves cannot change it, even with the best intentions. But Christ can change it if we trust him and give ourselves unconditionally to him.

Rom. 8:5 "Those who live on the level of their lower nature have their outlook formed by it." We experience this

again and again: people whose outlook is based on their lower nature come forth with hatred, jealousy, and envy – as if Christ had not come, as if he had not died on the cross, as if his sacrifice was in vain. This is extremely painful. Paul says, "The outlook of the
Rom. 8:7–8 lower nature is enmity with God. It is not subject to the law of God; indeed it cannot be: those who live on such a level cannot possibly please God." It cannot be put more strongly: those who cannot overcome their desires may mean no evil, but in actual fact their lives are hostile to God. They are not subject to his law. This goes for anyone who lives in impurity, hatred, jealousy, deceit, or other sinfulness. It is impossible for him to please God.

Rom. 8 Paul speaks in Romans 8 about the lower or fleshly nature, and we must be clear that this includes our desires for food, comfort, and sex. All must be subject to the Spirit. We need food and housing, and we affirm sex within marriage, but if these things rule us instead of Christ, we are sinning. God knows that we need food on the table every day, but that must not rule us; we must not become dependent on good food or spoil our children and ourselves. Food is just a simple example, of course. If we are ruled by *anything* but Christ, even spiritual things – religious thinking and reading – we are living by the flesh. Even if we were to adhere to the most self-mortifying philosophy, like that of the Buddha, it would still be fleshly, because we would be blowing up our pride by putting ourselves in the center instead of Christ.

Everything depends on whether we are completely given over to Christ. Romans 8:9 says that he who does not have the spirit of Christ is not even a Christian. Yet we cannot acquire it ourselves; we can only receive it by giving ourselves to him. The Gospel says that "everyone who asks receives…to him who knocks, the door will be opened." In other words, he who asks will receive living water without needing to pay anything.

Rom. 8:9

Mt. 7:7–8

We have great compassion with people who struggle in vain, year in and year out, to overcome their weaknesses, but at the same time we must admit that actually they are guilty. There is no excuse for them, because they do not give themselves in faith to Christ. As Paul writes, "There is no condemnation for those who are united with Christ Jesus, because in him the life-giving law of the Spirit has set us free from the law of sin and death." This possibility is open to everyone. We cannot hide from God and say, "We are too weak," or "We want to change, but cannot." Ultimately these excuses have no foundation. Paul continues:

Rom. 8:1–2

Rom. 8:12–13

> It follows, my friends, that our lower nature has no claim upon us; we are not obliged to live on that

> level. If you do so, you must die. But if by the Spirit you put to death all the base pursuits of the body, you will live.

These are very strong words. Who can really say that the lower nature has no claim on him? Such freedom from sin depends on absolute dedication to Christ. We must put to death every form of sin. Then it will be impossible for jealousy, hatred, impurity, lying, or any other sin to be victorious in us.

There are people who do not break with sin because they think they cannot. But that is an untruth. Jesus Christ is always there, and so is the Holy Spirit, and if any soul really cries out to God, the Spirit will speak to God for him. So there is no excuse whatsoever not to stop sinning. There is no one who has as much compassion and love for sinners as Jesus, but he does not excuse sin. Let us plead that everyone may find freedom from sin in Christ Jesus.

Rom. 8:26–27

Self-pity and pride, which are closely related, have nothing to do with the cross. Both of them are concerned only with me, me, me. We must turn away from them, otherwise we cannot experience complete victory over our sinfulness. It is said that in the time of the early church, the demons cried out, "Who is he that robs us of our power?" The believers answered with the exultant shout of victory, "Christ, the crucified!"* That should be our proclamation.

Jn. 13:34 "Love one another" is one of the most important commandments of Jesus, and we cannot take it seriously enough. There are other commandments that we must obey too: we should not love money; we should not commit adultery; we should not defile the flesh; and there are many other sins we must avoid. Yet Christ's greatest command is love. And therefore I think lovelessness is the greatest sin.

God will judge all forms of lovelessness, but especially contempt – the act of making someone believe he is a
Mt. 5:22 fool. Christ says, "Anyone who nurses anger against his brother must be brought to judgment…and if he sneers at him, he will have to answer for it in the fires of hell." Who has never been angry with his brother, or never sneered at him? Who has never spoken degradingly of another? Christ challenges us to live in perfect love.

From a letter: I feel guilty of being too harsh and even angry at times with my brothers and sisters. We

---

*Eberhard Arnold, ed., *The Early Christians* (Rifton, NY: Plough, 1997), p. 6.

must learn from Jesus how to be kind and gentle. On the other hand, we must never be wishy-washy; our compassion must always be mixed with the salt of Christ.

Jn. 17:15–16

The idea that we are "in the world" but not "of the world" cannot be understood by the intellect alone. Certainly, we will remain in the world as long as we live. But we are not to be "of it." Some people say dancing is "of the world" or "of the flesh." Others say it is worldly to wear short dresses. Still others say that alcohol is worldly, or that certain music or certain cars are. There are many so-called worldly things. If we are living in the Holy Spirit, we will feel in our hearts those things of the world which we must give up. May we not desire what is of the flesh; but may we be saved from making rules and regulations to prevent worldliness! May God show us what is of the Holy Spirit and what is of the spirit of the world.

If we had only the law, we could still hate someone even if we didn't kill him; we could still think evil thoughts of someone without shedding blood. But

Rom. 7:22–25

that is not enough. As Paul rightly says, the law can never change our hearts. It is Jesus who must live in us. Through him we can love our enemy, and through him we can fill our hearts with thoughts of God.

From a letter: You need to become absolutely determined to follow Jesus. It is not true that you are too weak to overcome sin – that is a lie of the devil. In Jesus it *is* possible to overcome sin. That is why he died on the cross. Live totally for him.

Mt. 5:6 – 8 "Blessed are those who hunger and thirst for justice, blessed are those who are merciful, blessed are those who are pure in heart." To be pure in heart is perhaps the hardest. It is easier to hunger and thirst for righteousness or to be compassionate or merciful. We ourselves cannot make our hearts pure.

Mt. 18:3 Only children have pure hearts, and therefore Jesus says that we must become like children. Yet we know that even if we strive to become like children, things that are not of God – impurity, envy, and vanity – enter our hearts continually, and so we need to be purified again and again by Christ.

Confession

From a letter: I have deep understanding for anyone who feels oppressed and burdened by sins of the past and has a longing to confess them. But confession itself is no help. People pay a lot of money to tell psychiatrists all their sufferings and sins, and these psychiatrists help them to find ways of quietening their consciences. But psychiatry alone does not bring true freedom.

You say you have confessed your sins but not found freedom. You will find it only when you confess your sins in faith: faith in God and in the cross of Jesus Christ, who died for the world's sins. All other confession consists of simply unloading your burdens onto another person, and later the burden will just come back. Peace is found only by those for whom confession of sins is bound together with a living faith. I wish you this faith.

With regard to confession: every conscious sin should be confessed, but this does not mean digging in the subconscious for every little thing. Where God tells us through our conscience that something is wrong, we should confess it and clear it up so that it can be forgiven. But confession should not make us self-centered; we want to find Jesus, not ourselves.

From a letter: You ask which evil thoughts one ought to confess. Every human being has thoughts come to
Mt. 16:23 him to which he must say, "Get behind me, Satan!" If you meet evil thoughts with this attitude you do not need to confess them, though you should forget them as soon as possible. Even if you have to fight against an evil thought for some moments before you reject it, you do not necessarily have to confess it. But if you give in to an evil thought and let it become part of

you, you should confess it. I would advise you not to occupy yourself too long with your thoughts.

From a letter: I uphold the sanctity of private confession in the fear of God, and I do not think it right if people who unburden their sins are then labeled because of them. However, in keeping the secrecy of confession, there is a point at which I would be sinning if I kept what I heard to myself. Should a member of the church commit a serious sin such as adultery I would feel I was betraying God if I kept quiet about it.

Spiritual Pride

The Bible says we must fight against the flesh, and people usually understand this to mean our sexuality, or perhaps excessive food and drink. But that is not the only meaning of the word "flesh." Certainly, sexual impurity and a luxurious lifestyle are "of the flesh," but so is the ego, and so is spiritual pride and everything else in us that is not of Christ.

We must ask God that the flesh in us – particularly our pride – may die. If we are proud, God cannot come to us. Pride is the worst form of the flesh, because it leaves no room in the heart for God.

Mt. 6:1–5 Jesus warns us very sharply against false piety–against wanting to be seen by others as "spiritual" or "good." All who want such recognition will find no reward in heaven. In being honored by others they have their reward already now. The same applies to people who do deeds of love and make a show of it. Christ says Mt. 6:3 that the left hand should not know what the right hand does.

We all have within us the desire to be liked, respected, or honored for our goodness. But Jesus warns us against this temptation and says that our piety should not be paraded before men. God sees what is hidden, and he will reward it.

As soon as we feel that we are something special or that we have something special to represent to others, we are in danger of losing everything we have received from God. No matter what we have experienced of God, we ourselves are still spiritually poor. There is a Lk. 6:24–25 religious truth in Jesus' words, "Woe to the rich; woe to those who have much." As soon as we hold to our own recognitions of truth instead of to the living God, our religious experience will become like a cold stone in our hands. Even the deepest or richest spiritual experience will die if it becomes a thing in itself.

From a letter: Dear brother, you have been proud of your work; you have thought little of your brothers and sisters, and you have lived in false humility, which is the deadliest form of spiritual pride. There is no question that you are gifted, that you are strong, that you are smart, and that you can get a lot done, but that is not the issue. We do not live together on account of these gifts. They are all mortal and will pass away. What lasts forever is humility and love–love, the incorruptible "treasure in heaven" of which Jesus speaks in the Sermon on the Mount.

Mt. 5–7

Mt. 11:18–19

When John the Baptist did not eat, the people despised him, and when Jesus ate and drank, they despised him too. Looking at one's brothers and sisters as if through a microscope to find something to criticize can bring complete destruction to a community. Let us not expect of others what we do not expect of ourselves.

From a letter: Dear sister, turn away from your opinionatedness and your need to be in the right. How different things would be if you had a humble, listening ear. When we speak, let us be open to the heart of the other. Let us share with one another and listen to one another. Ultimately we have to see that we are all stumbling blocks. Only God is good.

From a letter: Your way of judging people to be either great or insignificant, weak or strong, is completely
1 Cor. 2:1–5 unchristian. Do you think the apostles were strong? They were poor in spirit. Peter was without doubt a coward when he denied Jesus three times, and his story has been told through all the centuries. He was not ashamed that his betrayal was recorded in each of the Gospels, even though he repented for it his whole life long. You want to be great; you want to be strong, but by it you do an injustice to your brothers and sisters.

When Jesus comes close to people, he looks at what is in their hearts. He has compassion with the sinner. But he never calls sin good; he judges it. You must cleanse your heart of all critical thoughts, all jealousy, and all hatred, and you must stop classifying people. I think of you with great love.

From a letter: Do not fear that you can never be freed from pride and envy. You can be freed. But first you must see how much greater Jesus is than all your sins, and then he can take them away. Ask yourself, "What is there still in me that hinders Jesus from overwhelming me fully?" For Jesus to fill your heart, it must first be empty. Read the Beatitudes: they begin
Mt. 5:3–12 with "Blessed are the poor in spirit." That means becoming completely empty and powerless before Jesus.

From a letter: The more deeply you recognize that your pride cuts you off from God, the deeper the peace you will find. The pride you have in your wealth of knowledge is your greatest enemy. If only you would recognize how poor and miserable you actually are, dear brother, and how wretched you are in your sin! I wish you true repentance.

From a letter: I cannot say it strongly enough: your spiritual pride – your listening to God's Word in order to be exalted, instead of to be judged and given new life – is completely opposed to the way of Jesus. Give up your religious vanity. It leads to death.

From a letter: I believe that your bondage to sin has its roots in a terrible self-righteousness and pride. When you see little wrongs in others you feel spiritually great. It should be the other way around. As Christians we should be lowly and remember that whoever is forgiven much loves much. (cf. Lk. 7:47) Pride is a poisonous root that draws love to itself and away from Jesus and our brothers. If we are humble, the root will die, because it will find no food and water in our hearts.

In Paul's time some believers proclaimed Christ out of jealousy and a quarrelsome spirit, not out of goodwill. (Phil. 1:15) This was terrible, and it came about because they wanted human honor. Let us become humble and recognize that all human honor takes honor away from God, to whom alone it belongs. Let us honor no one but God, and let us never accept honor for ourselves.

What matters is that God works in us, inspiring both our will and deed. For him to do this we must give ourselves to him and give up all self-glory and honor.

Self

Those whose thoughts turn only around themselves forget that Christianity has an objective content. Christianity is a cause for which a person must completely forget himself and his little ego.

When we put ourselves in the center we make God out to be very small. It is important to recognize that he exists even without us. His cause is so very much greater than our existence. It is wonderful if we are used for God's cause, but it would exist even if we were not there.

The best way to experience nothing is to keep looking into yourself. But the more you are able to look outward and forget yourself, the more you can be changed by God. There are some people (and I have great pity on them) who are inclined to watch themselves constantly, as if in a mirror, and because of this they are often unnecessarily tense and cannot hear what God is saying to them.

We cannot redeem ourselves or better ourselves in our own strength. All we can do is to give ourselves completely to God. When we give ourselves to him without reserve, he helps us. That is our faith, our
Rom. 5:6–8 belief, and our experience. Self-redemption is out of the question, and here we must recognize the limitations of psychology and psychiatry. We do not reject them completely, but they are limited. God is far greater.

From a letter: If you look at yourself honestly you will see pride, impurity, selfishness, and all kinds of evil. Don't look at yourself. Look to Christ. There you will find a perfect character.

From a letter: Turn away from yourself, the fear of your sin, and your fear of having possibly sinned. Open yourself to God and his church. He is not so unmerciful that you need to live in constant fear.

You are inclined to analyze and judge yourself in a way that does not free you. There is a sense in which judging yourself can make you free: Paul says
1 Cor. 11:31 that he who judges himself will not be judged. But there is a certain self-judgment which brings terrible depression and leads away from God. The difference lies in whether or not you have a childlike faith in Jesus Christ, who wants to free us from all sin. Judge yourself in this faith and there will be a blessing on it.

The way you are judging yourself now could make you mentally ill and even lead to complete disaster.

It may be that you have a strong inclination to this or that sin, but every person has this tendency to some extent–and every person has to die to it. Everything depends on believing that Christ died for your sins. Read Hebrews 5:7–9 with a childlike heart:

Heb. 5:7–9

> In the days of Christ's earthly life he offered up prayers and petitions with loud cries and tears to God, who was able to deliver him from the grave. Because of his humble submission, his prayer was heard: Son though he was, he learned obedience in the school of suffering, and, once perfected, became the source of eternal salvation for all who obey him.

If you really believe this, you can find healing.

From a letter: If we think of how much Jesus does for us each day, it should keep us faithfully seeking him again and again. You feel you have nothing to give Jesus in return. But even if you have to recognize your selfishness and your lack of love, I do not think your depression is right. The early Christians said that there is a sorrow that leads to God and a sorrow that leads to the devil. If you think deeply about these words, you will turn from all depression that hinders love.

From a letter: Please give up your wanting to be loved. It is the opposite of Christianity. The prayer of St. Francis says, "Grant that I may not so much seek to be loved as to love." As long as you seek to be loved, you will never find peace. You will always find reasons for envy, but its real root is self-love. It is your wanting to be loved that is your downfall. You *can* change; there is no reason for despair. But you must learn to love your neighbor as yourself.

Purity

Mt. 5:8 *From a letter:* Jesus says, "Blessed are the pure of heart." This is the only answer to your question about relationships between young men and women. The fight against the Tempter goes on everywhere. Jesus
Mt. 5:27–29 says we should rather pluck out an eye than look lustfully at a woman. Only this attitude can give us a pure heart. We cannot make our hearts pure with our own efforts, but we can take this attitude, and then God will help us to victory.

Purity of heart comes as a gift from God, and the
1 Cor. 6:9–11 church must fight to protect it. We oppose lust just as much as we oppose private property and the spirit of murder. Purity is God's will, and every wedding in the church must be a testimony to it, as also the life of every member. Purity is a blessing. Whether it is given in a marriage or to a single person, a great grace lies on a pure life.

We must not underestimate the armies of impure spirits that drive man to evil. When we play with impurity, we put ourselves under the dominion of demons, and our sexuality – which is meant to be a wonderful experience of God – becomes a terrible and life-destroying experience. This is true not only in prostitution, but also when a person satisfies himself through committing impure acts on his own body. A man should not think he can indulge in masturbation without suffering harm from it; he hurts God and himself in doing so. He allows evil spirits to dwell within him–devils of whose cruel character he has no inkling–and an atmosphere of evil will come from him.

The blatant impurity shown on television and in magazines and movies is a publicly committed crime, and we must protest it. It ruins the souls of children and young people. Everything has become permissible–one thinks, for instance, of how homosexual acts have been legalized–and it has done terrific harm to the purity of the young. Something in the conscience of man has been killed.

In the end, lust leads to murder–just think of the limitless numbers of abortions that have taken place since it became legal. And think of the mental agony that young girls and women suffer who are guilty of killing the child in their womb. The number of mental breakdowns that result from this are incalculable. Jesus is the only answer to all this, and we must unitedly testify to his way in a world that has grown very dark.

When a person gratifies sexual impulses on his own body, he harms his soul, which is made in God's image. It is desecration to employ something destined for a sublime end in a manner contrary to that destiny. In the same way that royalty would be debased by being enslaved, so man debases his noble destiny as an image of God when he abuses his own body sexually.

From a letter: Dear brother, it is not necessary for your whole life to be cramped up in a struggle for personal purity. But you must give up all secret attraction to impurity. That is where your inner cramping comes from. Jesus can free you completely of this. If you know you are utterly dependent on him, then there is hope for you.

From a letter: Dear sister, it seems to me that there is an atmosphere of eroticism around you, and I want to warn you about this. There is nothing surprising about the fact that the powers of eroticism and sex are problems any person has to face, and you are no different from anyone else. But I plead with you to value the gift of purity–the light of absolute chastity and virginity. Do not let the smallest shadow of an overly casual relationship with boys or men come into your life, also not in the way you dress or the way you walk. Please take this advice as from someone who loves you.

From a letter: Dear brother, you say you have not resisted evil, especially in the area of sex. It is of great importance that you take a stand for Jesus' sake. I know it is often hard to do, especially at college. But as the times become more and more corrupt, it will be necessary to have a strong character and say "No" to things which the general public approves of. I wish you the courage to do this.

From a letter: You must seek a pure heart. Then you will stop sinning when impure images or your imagination or anything else tempts you.

You recognize that you must break away from these things, but you also acknowledge that you were playing around with them. That is sinful. Apathy and indifference will only weaken your stand against temptation. In the end it boils down to whether or not your life is founded on Jesus. You will find a pure heart only in him.

Trust

Why is it so hard to believe Christ and trust him
completely? Christ wants to give us his life and spirit,
and if we look to him for only a moment, our hearts
tell us: Here is one we can trust. Yet each of us knows
feelings of fear and anxiety. Something in us seeks Christ,
and at the same time something in us wants to serve
self and is unwilling to surrender to him completely.
Jn. 14:1 But that is what we must do, for the Gospel says "trust
and believe." It is not enough to give Christ what is
good in us, or to give him our sins, or to bring him
our burdens. He wants our entire selves. If we do not
give ourselves to him completely – if we hold on to our
reservations – we will never find the full inner freedom
and peace promised in the Gospel. We must give Christ
our innermost being.

Often the power of darkness puts fear into our hearts
and keeps us from full dedication to God. When Jesus
Jn. 6:53 said in the synagogue, "Unless you eat my flesh and
drink my blood, you can have no life," even his followers
found these words hard to accept, and many of them
Jn. 6: 67–69 left him. But when Jesus asked the twelve, "Will you
also leave me?" Peter responded, "Lord, to whom shall
we go? You have the words of eternal life. We have faith,
and we know that you are the Holy One of God." Such
faith must live in us too – in our hearts, our souls, and
our whole being. It must become a reality in us again
and again: not a religious system, not a theory, but the
knowledge that we can trust Jesus completely and give

him everything – our whole lives – for all eternity. It is not necessary for us to understand everything intellectually. It is much more important to experience trust and faith in our hearts and being.

Jn. 14:27 Apart from Jesus we will find no peace. Where he is, there is God. He is there even for those who leave him, as did many people in his time who found his words too difficult to accept. Therefore we pray for ourselves and for them, "Lord, help us. Come into this world. We need thee, thy flesh, thy spirit, thy death and life, and thy message for the whole creation."

Mt. 10:26 – 31 We should fear neither our enemies nor the slander and persecution that may come to us. We should trust in Jesus. He was also slandered and persecuted. We do not want anything better. If we turn in complete trust and love to Jesus, I feel absolutely sure that we will be kept under the loving protection of God.

We must believe and trust that Jesus is the answer to all our perplexities, problems, and anxieties. I have not always trusted Jesus enough, but I recognize my lack of trust as sin. Life is not without perplexities or anxieties. Yet we know where to turn. It is very simple: if you don't understand something, trust Jesus. This is not always easy; sometimes it costs an inner fight to do so wholeheartedly. But Jesus says, "Trust in God and trust also in me." That is the only answer.

Jn. 14:1

From a letter: I would advise you not to puzzle too much about difficult questions of faith, such as why God might use a man whom he loves as a tool of his wrath. We do not know enough about God's love. The only answer to such questions is complete, unconditional trust.

From a letter: Even when we are in inner need we must forget ourselves and give ourselves in daily service to those around us. Then God will help us. It is not necessarily good for us to keep on talking about our problems or to share our difficulties again and again. God knows what we need before we ask him. Trust in him like a child. Then he will help you.

If we feel tempted to lose trust in each other because of struggles we have gone through, or for any other reason, we must find inner quiet. We must have an
Mt. 26:39 attitude of trusting dedication to Jesus that says, "not my will, but thy will" and makes us absolutely quiet inwardly. Without this strengthening trust, I personally could not go through one day. Churches and community groups like ours will pass away; we will all pass away. Ultimately, Jesus alone will be victor.

From a letter: I know from mothers of little children that they are sometimes afraid of the terrible things that may happen to their children in today's world. I can put myself in their shoes very well. My first children were born during the bombing of England in World War II, when bombers passed over us every night. Twice bombs dropped nearby – one on our land, and one in the next village. But greater than our fear of bombs was our fear that Hitler would conquer England. For us adults that would have meant death, and it brought unspeakable inner need to me when I thought about what would happen to our children.

We are not living in fear of bombers now, but our time is one of great suffering and death. It is entirely possible that many of us – including parents of little children – may one day have to suffer and die for our faith. I beg you – from the depths of my heart – to trust God completely. There are many frightening passages
Rv. 21:4 in the Bible, especially in the Revelation of John. But even there it says that God himself will wipe away the tears of all those who have suffered. We must really believe that Jesus came not to bring judgment but to bring salvation:

Jn. 3:16–17

> God loved the world so much that he gave his only Son, that everyone who has faith in him may not die but have eternal life. It was not to judge the world that God sent his Son into the world, but that through him the world might be saved.

Here we see the indescribable longing of God to save humankind. At the end we shall be one with God. We must believe this, for our children too, even if we have to suffer for Jesus' sake.

Like sunshine over a valley, God's great love spreads out over the whole earth. It is true that there are terrible things in the world, such as war; and wars will come, but God is greater. He is much greater than man, and his love is much greater than man's. Do not live in fear. Look down across the valley and toward the mountains, and think of the great God who created all things, and who has you in his hand.

If we live according to Jesus and his teachings, we have no reason to be afraid. Let us be faithful to him and to God and leave all fear behind.

Learn to trust Jesus always, even when you cannot understand something. Situations will often arise in life without your understanding why. The only answer is to trust Jesus.

You will go through very hard times, but never forget that the final victory is God's. Always believe
Rv. 21:1 this. Heaven and earth shall pass away, but a new heaven and a new earth are coming.

Reverence

We should fear God, and we should fear hurting or offending anything created, but we should not be afraid of God. The Bible speaks of the fear of God, but there is a different fear that leads away from God and makes love grow cold. Woe to us if we confuse the right fear with the wrong. Our fear should be born of love and reverence.

When Peter recognized Jesus as the Son of God
Lk. 5:8 he said, "Depart from me; I am a sinful man." He was afraid to be confronted with the purity of Jesus. Such fear is right. But fear that takes away trust and confidence or destroys one's childlikeness is wrong. We must fear God in the right way.

1 Jn. 4:18 *From a letter:* John writes that he who has fear is not perfect in love. This has given me much food for thought, because several of the parables of Jesus, like
Mt. 25:1–13 that of the ten virgins, could make one fearful. The Book of Revelation, too, can be frightening. And Jesus
Mt. 10:28 says that even though we should not fear men who can kill the body, we should fear him who can destroy both soul and body in hell. So there is a fear of God that is right and good. Ultimately, if we are in God we will fear nothing but God. That is the perfect state for a Christian.

We have always been reserved in using the name of God, not only because our own inner feeling makes us cautious but because the Ten Commandments say:
Ex. 20:7 "You shall not use the name of the Lord your God in vain." It is important for parents to teach their children to respect God so that misusing his name will not even come into question for them.

Dt. 4:5–9 People are so terribly inclined to forget God and his deeds of love. That is the worst thing that can happen to humankind. When no one is interested in God any longer – when no one wants to know about him or testify to him – it is even worse than being hostile toward him, because hostility at least shows an interest.

Lk. 2:25–39 We should be stimulated by the story of Simeon and Anna, who expected the Messiah on behalf of the whole people of Israel. It does not matter if there are only two – for even then the earth has not entirely forgotten God. We should be eager to testify to him, to love him, and to expect his coming.

Surrender

Despite the circumstances of our time we must be open and free to live for God's will for the future – for brotherly community and the kingdom of God. We must be ready and willing to give up our resistance to God; then he will work in us through his Holy Spirit.

God is always ready, always there. It is we who are not ready for his cause. If we would only yield to God's authority, to the way of Jesus, and to the power of the Spirit, then the flame which gives light to the whole world could be kindled.

Mt. 19:21 We know Jesus' commands: "Leave everything you
Mt. 8:22 have, and come follow me! Sell all your possessions."
Mt. 4:19–20 "Do not wait to bury your father." "Leave your fishing
boat and your tools and come with me!"

The disciples, too, knew Jesus' commands. They also
Mt. 19:23–26 knew that every man – each in his own way – is "rich"
enough to resist them by holding on even to the little
Lk. 14:20 he has; to tell Jesus, "I cannot come." That is why they
asked, horrified, "Then how can anyone be saved?" Jesus answered, "It is impossible for men. But with God all things are possible."

If we open ourselves to God's working and give up our self-will, he is always ready to give us faith and love.

Mt. 7:7–11

God wants us to ask him for help. It is not that he cannot or does not want to act without our asking, but he waits for us to open our hearts and lives so that he and only he can act.

Many people ponder why God is like this, why he doesn't force his will on men. But that is how God is. He waits for our readiness. It is true that he punishes individuals and nations to call them to repentance, but he never forces his goodness on them. If a parent were to take his child by the throat and force his good intentions on him, the child would instinctively feel that this was not love. For the same reason, God does not force his will on anyone. So we are confronted by a momentous question: Are we willing to surrender ourselves to God voluntarily? Are we willing to open the windows of our hearts so that God in his goodness can enter and take over?

We have to give ourselves wholeheartedly to God, and if we fail, we must give ourselves again. We all need daily forgiveness for our sins and failures. But what matters is whether we want to be faithful – faithful to the end of our lives. This means surrendering everything – our self-will, our hopes for personal happiness, our private property, even our weaknesses – and believing in God and in Christ. That is all that is asked of anyone. Jesus does not expect perfection, but he wants us to give ourselves wholeheartedly.

From a letter: What is true and unconditional surrender? A person may yield to a stronger person, or an army to a stronger army. One may yield to God because he is almighty, or because one fears his judgment. None of this is full surrender. Only if one experiences that God is good – and that he alone is good – is it possible to surrender to him unconditionally one's whole heart, soul, and being.

When a person has surrendered to God with heart and soul, he will then seek others in whom the same love is clearly expressed and surrender to them also. But he can commit himself to others only if his first commitment is to God.

From a letter: If we ever found a group – even if it were a much smaller group than ours – where the love of Jesus was expressed more fully and clearly than it is among us, I hope and believe that we would want to join them, even if it meant losing our particular culture or identity.

From a letter: God must lead us to the point where we recognize how wretched and weak we are – yes, how poor in spirit and completely helpless. Whoever
2 Cor. 12:1–11 feels even the least bit strong must have his weakness revealed to him. When God shows us how wretched and poor we actually are, we feel completely helpless

before him. But then he helps us with his grace and strengthens us with his unending love. We are absolutely dependent on God, on Christ, and on the Holy Spirit. There is no other help.

Surrendering to the will of Jesus means becoming one with him and with one another. Jesus fought so hard to surrender his will to the Father's that he sweated drops of blood. Evil powers surrounded him and tried to cause his downfall, but he remained faithful: his attitude was "Thy will, not my will." This should be our attitude, too, in all questions, even if we are persecuted for our faith. Whatever happens, imprisonment or even death, we should say, "Thy will, not my will."

Lk. 22:42

Submission

Jn. 15:16

Christ says, "You did not choose me; I chose you. I appointed you and put you in your place; you shall go and bear fruit, fruit that shall last." This is so very important: "I put you in your place."* How often a person causes terrible harm when he is not satisfied with his place in life. Such dissatisfaction leads to hatred. We should love one another and accept the place God has given each of us.

*This phrase, although omitted in most English versions of the Bible, is in several German ones. See Albrecht, *Das Neue Testament* (Giessen, 1972, 10th ed.).

Mt. 21:1–7

When Jesus sent two disciples to fetch a donkey's colt on Palm Sunday, they had no other task in the whole world more important than fetching it. If someone had said to them, "You are called to greater things; anyone can fetch a donkey," and they had not done it, they would have been disobedient. But there was nothing greater for them at that moment than to fetch the donkey for Christ. For myself and for each individual I wish that we might do every task, great or small, in this obedience. There is nothing greater than obedience to Christ.

Humility

Jesus calls each of us to be humble. If a person seeks human greatness, Christian community is not the place for him. Any one of us might be tempted by ambition, but we must take an attitude against such temptation.

From a letter: It is good to be weak. Our human weakness is no hindrance to the kingdom of God, as long as we do not use it as an excuse for our sins. Read 2 Corinthians 12:7–9, where Paul writes that the Lord will show himself in the most glorious way through our weakness. Certainly this is not the most important passage for the church as a whole, but it is perhaps the most important passage in the Bible as regards personal discipleship.

2 Cor. 12:7–9

From a letter: In reading the Gospel of Mark, I have been struck by how Jesus emphasizes our need for humility. He did not come to be served but "to serve
Mk. 10:45 and to give his life as a ransom for many." This must be our way too, even though we know we fall very short of fulfilling it.

Mt. 5:3–12 The Beatitudes do not call for great saints who shine in the world, but for lowly people.

From a letter: If you know you are sometimes critical and lack humility, then seek humility. Humility is a virtue that one can decide for. It softens the heart and makes a person open for God. Criticism is not necessarily wrong; it can be positive. But it can also be very destructive.

We should not think too much about our small hearts or our weak characters. No one is pure and good except Jesus. His is the only really healthy character, and in his unending mercy, he can purify our hearts for his purpose. Let us give ourselves to him so he can lead us and use us as he will. Let us turn our back
Gn. 4:5 on the temptation of Cain, who envied his brother's closeness to God. Let us be joyful in simply belonging to Jesus, and willing to let him place us where we can bear the most fruit to the glory of God.

From a letter: If we accept the weakness and smallness of our lives in a way that leads us to humility before God, we will recognize that our only help lies in complete surrender to him and dependence on him. It might be a very painful recognition, but the victory will be life!

Phil. 2:3 Paul says, "There must be no room for rivalry and personal vanity among you." He does not only mean the vanity of wanting to look beautiful – which is also unchristian – but the religious vanity of people who want to shine among men and be honored by them. There should be no room for such vanity among us. He continues, "You must humbly reckon others better than yourselves." That is the opposite of wanting to outshine one's brother or sister. If we want to follow Jesus, how can we want to make ourselves great or
Phil. 2:8 important? Jesus "humbled himself, and in obedience accepted even death – death on a cross."

Sincerity

How important it is that our life is genuine and remains genuine, and that we do no more – but also not the least bit less – than God requires of us at any moment! There is a danger of coming to an intellectual recognition of the truth and then living a life that conforms to it, when the truth is not yet actually given by God into our hearts and souls.

Mt. 7:21

Let us never use religious words when we do not mean them. If we speak admiringly about discipleship but resist its demands at the same time, it will harm our soul and our inner life. Let us be reserved with religious terms and expressions of faith. Using them without meaning them will destroy us – and our hypocrisy will be especially disastrous for our children.

Mt. 6:5

Jesus warns us sharply against trying to appear devout in other people's eyes. Let us be genuine and say what we truly think, even if we are off the mark, rather than use the right words without meaning them.

From a letter: According to old Jewish tradition, the high priest uses the name Jehovah only once a year – on the Day of Atonement – and then only in the Holy of Holies in the temple. For us, such reverence in the use of religious words is an important form of inner chastity. We are very cautious in using God's name.

From a letter: It is important to be straightforward and honest about your true feelings. Rather be too rude than too smooth, too blunt than too kind. Rather say an unkind word that is true than one that is "nice" but untrue. You can always be sorry for an unkind word, but hypocrisy causes permanent harm unless special grace is given.

The Youth Movement, in which our community has its roots, was marked by a search for what was genuine, and though it was not a "religious" movement, there was something of Jesus alive in it.* The first question people asked was not whether a thing was right, good, or true, but whether it was genuine. They preferred to have someone innocently say something incorrect or awkward than to have to listen to insincere religious

*The German Youth Movement, or *Jugendbewegung,* a widespread phenomenon of loosely organized youth groups, was active mainly from 1913 to 1933 and rejected the established conventions of society in favor of simplicity, freedom, genuineness, and a love of nature. Eberhard Arnold, who founded the Bruderhof in 1920, was a nationally-known writer, speaker, and leader in this movement.

speeches. They rejected parrotlike religion; they struggled to find the truth.

From deep within people's hearts there arose a new approach to life, a new feeling for life that expressed itself in many ways. This inward urge led to fellowship in hiking, singing, and folk dancing, and even in communal settlements. A gathering around a blazing fire became a deeply-felt inner experience, and the rhythmic movement of a circle dance brought to expression something from the depths of the heart. There was an effort to give shape only to what was truly genuine, and it meant rejecting all human pretense, including fashion. The inner experience was all-important, and it found vivid expression in every area of life.

From a letter: It is not the obvious sinner who stands in the way of God. God's greatest enemies are those who receive and accept Christ's call to discipleship but then – despite their use of religious language – continue to serve Satan at the same time.

Most of Jesus' parables deal with such people, not
Mt. 25:1–13 with people of the world. The ten virgins in Matthew
25 all go out to seek the bridegroom, but five of them
Mt. 24:48–49 fall asleep; and in Matthew 24:48–49 the servant is
appointed by his master but becomes unfaithful, and so on. That is what hinders God's kingdom the most: when those who have heard his call and answered it go on to serve Satan while still using Christian words.

If we stay close to Jesus, we will find genuineness in its
Mt. 23:26–28 clearest form. How sharply he speaks against the piety that tries to cleanse from the outside! How clearly he tells us that the inside must first be cleansed!

The Church

The Church

We know humankind is tormented and divided. Part of this torment is loneliness, which can be overcome only by experiencing the living church. This church cannot be identified with a specific group or organization, but it does exist; it lives and comes down to
Eph. 1:22–23 humble, seeking people. The fact that the church exists is the most important reality on earth. When God speaks in the innermost chamber of our hearts, our sinful separation and loneliness are overcome; we experience inner community with our brothers and sisters.

We cannot say that the church is here or there. The church comes down from heaven to those who are spiritually poor. It comes to those who give up all things for Christ's sake, including their own ideas and rights. This can happen anywhere, and when it does it always brings people together in unity.

According to the early Christians, the church existed even before creation. It exists in the Holy Spirit. Christ sends the church wherever two or three meet together in his name–and wherever they give up all rights, power, property, and self for him.

When we are asked whether we are the church, we have to say, "No, we are not the church." But when we are asked whether the church comes to us, we have to testify that it does, especially if we are broken and poor before God. The poorer a group is spiritually, the closer the church can come to it. Our own ideas, especially the idea of having influence or power over other people, must be given up completely. We must become poor as beggars before God.

If we speak of the true church, we certainly do not mean ours. We simply mean all those who live their lives in full unity with Christ. Only the fruits can show where this is.

In the writings of the early Christians, for instance in Hermas' *The Shepherd,* we find the thought that the church existed before anything was created: "Because the church was created before all other things, she is old. It was for her sake that the world was formed."* It is a deep and remarkable thought – a complete contrast to the idea of a little congregation or even a gathering of millions of people calling themselves the church.

When we speak of our community as a church, we certainly do not mean to imply that it is *the* church. The church is something far greater. It goes back to the beginning of all things, before the creation of the world. But we long that it is at work today, also among us.

---

*Eberhard Arnold, ed., *The Early Christians* (Rifton, NY: Plough, 1997), p. 310 ff.

The 16th century Anabaptist Peter Riedemann compares the gathering of believers in the church to a lantern. A lantern is of no use unless there is a light in it. The same is true for the church. It may hold all goods in common, with no private property; it may have love, complete dedication, and true community. But that does not guarantee it is alive. The church is a gift from God. It comes to the spiritually poor, and it is united and enlivened by the Holy Spirit.

From a letter: In this hour of world need and world despair there is nothing more important than a life of brotherhood, a life of unity and love. It may be so small in comparison to the whole of world need that it is almost invisible, but it will have an effect.

People today do not need long sermons or religious words; they need to be shown deeds and a practical
1 Pt. 2:12 way of discipleship. Our time needs the tangible demonstration that God is stronger than all hate, all need, all sin, and all disunity.

God needs a people who devote their lives completely, without reservation, to his cause. They should be people who do not consider their own salvation first but who intercede in prayer for the needs of men and hope and believe in the victory of God.

A true community cannot exist for a single day without the gift of the Holy Spirit. Therefore, whether in our being together in silence or in singing, we expect and await this gift which God has offered us through the death of Jesus.

Acts 4:32 It is said that the early church was of one heart and one soul. It may not have been a well-organized body, but it was of one heart and one soul. Its members were moved by the Spirit from above, and through this movement it came about that they held everything in common, and no one called anything his own. It was not a matter of cold law – not organized communism – but a matter of moved hearts.

From a letter: It is not we who can build brotherhood – not we who can found a church or change even a single human being. We are all completely dependent on the atmosphere or spirit of God ruling among us. Yet at the same time we all have an influence on this atmosphere, and so it is the responsibility of each of us to see that no spirit opposed to God is allowed to come into our lives.

If we are faithful to Jesus, we will also be faithful to one another. We belong to one another. If someone dedicates himself to Jesus, he will be united with other believers, and they will become so united that they
1 Cor. 12:12–27 are like one body. In the human body, if anything threatens the eye, the arm will move quickly to protect it, even if it is injured in doing so. This happens

automatically, as if out of love. It is the same among those who dedicate themselves to Christ and to each other. Each should be willing to suffer for the other – the stronger one for the weaker.

From a letter: In Jesus and his spirit we all become one, even one with the church in heaven, with the apostles and martyrs, and with all those who have been and are one with Jesus. But if our love shifts away from Jesus, the Redeemer and Savior of the world, then even our faith in the church becomes idolatry.

It is a paradox: we must separate ourselves from our corrupt generation – and we cannot do that sharply enough – but we must also unite with Christ, who died for every individual of this same generation. What we as a church need most is to find the crucified Christ, the Lamb of God who died for the sins of the world. If we are united with Christ, we will not be cold-hearted, whether toward a girl who has had an abortion or to anyone else who does any other evil; we will have compassionate hearts.

From a letter: Our community has certain characteristics which arise partly from its European background and other historical circumstances. The same is true of the Church of the Brethren, the Quakers, or other religious movements. I can well understand that people feel a certain love and attachment to the culture and, still more, the people of their background.

But let us consider for a moment the "community of believers," the Body of Christ that has continued through all the centuries. What is our church, then, with its culture? Whatever good there may be in it is there only insofar as it is surrendered to and gripped by this stream of life. Our community will pass away as many movements have passed away, but the stream of life of which it is a part can never pass away. That is what matters.

If we had made up our minds to be a Christian group of German culture, serving only those people with a background in the Youth Movement, we would have been in danger of drying up even before we began. We want to surrender our lives completely and allow ourselves to be used wherever God moves people's hearts, to be open to whatever God gives us. Otherwise we are in danger of limiting the truth.

We are only a weak circle of human beings–often all too human. But our task can never be limited. God is limitless.

The older I get, the less important my community is to me. The main thing is that God's praying church exists on this earth. It is for this that we want to give ourselves, and for this that we want to live.

We need to feel a certain inner urgency; we cannot let life pass by without giving ourselves completely to the church. The church was with God before the world was created, and it is now with God in heaven as the "upper church," the cloud of witnesses from every nation, tribe, and race. We cannot stand undecided before this holy reality.

From a letter: Are we as a church so dedicated, so full of truth and salt, that we are able to influence the whole earth in the way that even a pinch of salt flavors a whole dish of food? It is not enough to live together in community, to love one another and make each other happy; to make jam for our neighbor, who then makes jam for her neighbor. More is demanded.

I believe that we are living in the end time. It is a crucial hour. Everything depends on whether our
Mt. 25:1–13 lamps are trimmed, whether we are ready to meet the bridegroom. Jesus' farewell words in the Gospel of
Jn. 17:21 John make it clear: the church must be so united that the world can recognize God as the Father who sent Jesus. It shakes me to the depths of my heart to ask, Are we really showing this to the world?

Community

We must give up all private property and all thirst for collecting things for ourselves. The enjoyment of wealth for oneself, one's family, or even one's community leads to inner death. Wealth brings about death because it isolates the heart from God and from one's fellowman. We seek an answer to this in sharing everything in a way that makes it impossible to fall into the sin of collective wealth. Our door is open to everyone who seeks God and the truth. Under the stewardship of the church, everything is available to anybody in need.

Mt. 19:21 The way of Jesus means complete possessionlessness! We have chosen this way, and our children must know that from an early age. They should know that our money belongs to God and not to us. Jesus says we
Mt. 6:19–20 should not store up treasure for ourselves on earth, but seek our treasure in heaven.

From a letter: You ask, "How can we, as separate persons and families, become part of each other?" This has to be given by the spirit of Jesus. But first we must be completely emptied of our own ideas, ideals, and being; we must be there fully for Jesus and his spirit.

From a letter: There is no substitute for the actual experience of Christian community, the movement of God's spirit, and the unity of believers in the church. So I write this realizing that words can never contain the spirit of God's love, which moves among those who are surrendered to him in all things.

In answer to your question about the scriptural
Lk. 14:33 basis for our life, there is Luke 14:33, where Christ
states clearly that only those who renounce all that
Jn. 16:13 they have can be his disciples. There is also John 16:13,
which says that when the spirit of truth comes, he will
guide men into all truth. This occurred at Pentecost,
Acts 2:44 when the disciples were of one heart and one soul and
Acts 4:32–34 held all their goods in common. See also 1 Corinthians
1 Cor. 12:25–26 12, especially verses 25–26. We find it hard to take this
passage at full value in non-communal church life. The
2 Cor. 8:13–15 same is true of 2 Corinthians 8:13–15.

At Pentecost love overflowed from the hearts of those who were moved by the Spirit: the believers were full of love for God and for one another. I don't think
Acts 4:33 you would deny that "great grace was upon them all"
when this happened. Community of goods was the outcome of this love and grace. This communion of love is a far cry from the Christianity of today, when, for instance, people thankfully testify in their church paper that since they have started tithing, God has made their business prosper in a wonderful way.

It would be misrepresenting the facts to say that the main foundation of our belief is the sharing of money and possessions. That is an outcome of our faith, not its foundation. It is the fruit of full surrender to Christ and his love. We give back everything God has given us – our possessions, our talents, and our lives – to be controlled by him and his spirit alone.

In answer to your question whether this will help win souls to Christ, we would say no. Simply sharing goods does not necessarily lead to Christ. But when it is the result of overflowing love, it can lead to him. Many of our members come from unchristian backgrounds. It was the living-out of brotherhood and love that attracted us. We were tired of words; they are cheap and can be heard almost anywhere, for who will say that he is against brotherhood and love? We did not seek words, but deeds; not stones, but bread. That is what Christ offered – a new life where love rules everything, in deed and in truth.

You ask how much opportunity a convert has to spread the real Gospel, not the "community gospel." What do you mean by the Gospel? What does the "good news" mean if it doesn't mean that there is a way other than the way of death and despair that rules this present world? What is it if it isn't the news that men can live together as brothers in peace, in full trust and love to one another, and as children of one Father? The Gospel is not only words; it stands for deed and truth, for the whole way of life Christ has brought. It is the expression of a living experience. Our challenge is not to join our church, but to live in brotherhood. We do not wish to add anything to the Gospel, but we feel

strongly that nothing can be taken away from it, and
that we must face every demand it makes upon us.

You ask whether we as a community need to
isolate ourselves in order to be in the world but not
of it. We live apart only in the sense of separating
ourselves from the evil root of self-interest, greed, and
injustice – from all that is loveless in the present world
order. Society is basically no different today than it
was in Jesus' time. Men are still self-centered, proud,
and eager for their own gain, power, and position.
The fruits of this evil pervade society in many forms:
impurity, hatred, alcoholism, poverty, juvenile delin-
quency, mental illness, violent crime, and finally
1 Jn. 2:15–17 war. These are the fruits of mammon, the fruits of
an unchristian society, the fruits of the present world
order. This is the world out of which Christ called
and still calls us. He calls us out of it and brings us
together to build the city of God, where the Spirit
alone rules – to build the city on a hill, which cannot
be hidden but shines into the world.

The Gospels tell us that we will know a tree – or a
Mt. 7:16–18 person or a group – by its fruits, for a good tree cannot
produce evil fruit and an evil tree cannot produce
good fruit. The fruits of a life based on Christ are not
just preaching or speaking. It is our deeds that are
Jn. 13:35 important. Christ said all men would know we are his
Mt. 7:21 disciples by our love for one another – not by our *talk*
about loving one another. His last prayer was for the
Jn. 17:21 unity of his disciples: "May they all be one, even as
thou, Father, art in me, and I in thee; may they also

be in us, so the world may believe that thou hast sent me." So the church should be visible in the world. The light from the united body of believers must shine into the darkness of the world to the glory of God.

You ask, "If we deny ourselves enough to walk Christ's way, can't we live a sensible life amidst our fellowmen outside an organization of brothers?" You must answer this for yourself. We are here because we found that a "sensible life" was not enough – that Christ asked more of us. He wants the whole person. We are not an "organization of brothers" but simply a group of people who seek to live closer to God. We want to take Christ's words in the Sermon on the Mount literally and be measured and judged by them. We can only respond to them fully by surrendering our lives to his will in the faith that he will lead us to truth.

From a letter: Our communal life is a constant struggle: we must continually fight to break away from everything that separates us from God and from our brothers and sisters. This breaking away – this dying to ourselves – can be a most painful experience. We believe that one hundred percent is demanded of us; *all* pride and self-will must go, and the whole framework of life and thought in which we have tried to find security. This doesn't happen with a sudden burst of light, but only gradually. As we live together we recognize that certain things bring separation: pride, self-pity, and false piety. We must turn away from these evils as they are shown to us. We will always remain weak, but our joy is in finding a source of strength that can be victorious in every struggle.

Ps. 133 *From a letter:* It is a great gift to live with brothers and sisters. When God's love burns in us and welds us together to persevere in solidarity, no difficulty or struggle is too great. It is a relief to know that the life of discipleship is never something merely learned – not even through hard and painful struggle. Rather, it is a continually new experience of grace. What a deep paradox! The God of Abraham, of Isaac, and of Jacob is always the same, yet he alone frees us from monotony and law. In him everything is new.

We must always be aware of the danger of materialism – the rule of money or anything else material
Mt. 6:24 over our heart and soul. Jesus said, "You cannot serve two masters. You cannot serve God and mammon." In and of themselves material things are not the enemy; they are part of life. But they should be used for the tasks of the church. Ultimately it is a question of our attitude. The degeneration of the soul makes it possible for anything material to ruin a life. But if a person's relationship with Jesus and the church is alive, he will be able to use material things without being ruled by them.

From a letter: We are not interested in winning anyone with smooth words. Our way of communal life is much too demanding. Today we have house, home, work, and daily bread. But as the history of the Anabaptists, Quakers, and many other radical movements has shown us, we do not know what will happen tomorrow.

One enormous danger to the life lived in God, whether within community or not, is money–
Mt. 6:21 mammon. Jesus says, "Where your treasure is, there is your heart." The early Christian prophet Hermas speaks of the danger of owning fields, houses, and anything else of earthly value. He cries out: "Foolish, double-minded, wretched man, do you not realize that all these things do not belong to you, that they are under a power alien to your nature?"* In spite of the fact that we live in community of goods and share one purse, the danger of mammon still exists. Jesus says of
Lk. 9:58 himself: "The birds have nests, the foxes have holes; but the Son of Man has nowhere to lay his head."

*Eberhard Arnold, ed., *The Early Christians* (Rifton, NY: Plough, 1997), p. 317.

Can one bind oneself to a group of people? When our members take their vows we ask them, "Are you ready to surrender yourself unreservedly to God, to Christ, and to the brothers?" The question here is not surrender to God or Christ, but whether one can bind oneself to a group of people. I have been thinking about the meaning of the dedication spoken of here; this surrender to God, to Christ, and to brothers
Ex. 20:3 and sisters. We know the first commandment – have no other gods before God – and we know Christ's
Mt. 22:39 command to love our neighbor as ourselves. We
1 Jn. 4:20 also know that he who says he loves God but hates his brother is a liar. So we cannot separate our commitment to God from commitment to those of our fellowmen who also want to follow God.

On the other hand, it is dangerous to commit oneself without reservation to anyone; to commit oneself, as it says here, "to the brothers." What happens if those brothers go wrong, even in a subtle way? After the first and second generations religious groups may become rigid on certain points. They may become legalistic about things which seem right, and through this their inner life is suppressed.

If we see this danger, the real question is, "How can we bind ourselves to one another in spite of it?" The answer can be found only in faith in the Spirit – Christ's spirit. There is no other answer.

From a letter: I am grateful that you have openly confessed your negative thoughts and feelings toward other members of the church. God is stronger than likes and dislikes. He gives us love and he gives us community, where likes and dislikes are overcome.

From a letter: How well I understand that you are disappointed in our community. I, too, shudder when I think of all that has happened in our history. Yet ultimately it is not to a community or a church that we have given our lives, even though we vow to be faithful to our brothers and sisters. It is to Jesus that we have surrendered ourselves. He experienced betrayal. He experienced abandonment by all his disciples. He experienced godforsakenness. And still the Father's will was more important to him than anything else. So I hold firmly to that and challenge you also to hold firmly to it. In this hour when the Enemy has scattered
Mt. 12:30 so many, we must take Jesus' words to heart: "He who does not gather with me, scatters." My wish is to prove my faithfulness to Jesus and to my brothers and sisters by gathering with them.

If we want to live in church community we must do it for the sake of God alone. Otherwise, even with the best will, we will be like parasites on the inner life of the church. Even if we work more hours than other members, even if we produce more income than others, our efforts will lie like a heavy weight on the rest of the community. We have an open door for all people, but we also expect each one who wants to stay with us to accept the challenge of full discipleship. Otherwise our community will go to pieces.

Our witness to a life of complete community – to the fact that Jesus gathers and unites men – is fully in keeping with his words and his nature. But community itself is not decisive; the decisive thing is love. Community of work, community of goods, and the community of the common table are only fruits of this love.

From a letter: We are always thankful when God strengthens our community by giving us new members, but we do not want to "make" members with smooth words or try to convince anyone to join us by making a good impression. Communal life brings too much pain and need, and one cannot stand the test of its struggles if one does not trust wholly in God's strength. We do not have the strength in ourselves: God is the source of our strength.

Leadership

A true Christian church cannot be a living organism unless there is clear leadership. The ship of community needs a helmsman to guide it, and he must let himself be guided from above in deep humility and must honor and respect the brotherhood he leads. Being led from above means listening to the voice of the Holy Spirit as it speaks to the church as a whole. A leader must not isolate himself. Through close cooperation with all members, a perfectly clear direction in all matters can be found. This is true for all matters of faith, all practical things, and for the overall inner attitude of the church.

Any true service done for the church – including the service of leadership – is done as by an organ of the body, and it must therefore be done lovingly, sincerely, honestly, and in a childlike way. Someone who carries a responsibility is no higher than someone who does not: no one is higher, and no one is lower. We are all members of one body.

1 Pt. 5:1–4 True leadership means service, so it is a terrible thing to use it as a position of power over others. When such abuse of leadership takes place in a church community,

it is especially devilish, because brothers and sisters give themselves voluntarily, trustingly, and openheartedly to the church. In a dictatorial state, people might yield to a greater power even though their souls reject it as evil. But in a brotherhood of believers, where members trust their leaders, the misuse of power is real soul-murder.

When we ask brothers to lead the church, we must ask God that much is given to them. But we must also let them be themselves – as God made them. They should not be presumptuous; they should express only what is given them by God. We do not expect more. It would be disastrous if anyone were to feel himself pushed into a role that was not genuinely his. We do not expect someone who is meant to be an ear to be an eye.

When we speak about the authority of leaders in the church, it should be very clear that we never mean authority over people. Jesus gave his disciples authority, but he gave them authority over spirits – not people. In the same way, those of us appointed to lead the church are given authority, but not over people. It is all too easy to forget this. We must seek for humility again and again.

A servant of the Word* is always in danger of teaching something false or suppressing something of the truth. I have a great fear of this, and I ask you to intercede for
Acts 20:20–27 us all in prayer. Paul could say that he had neglected nothing and done everything in his duty as an apostle
Acts 23:1 of the church. This strikes me very deeply. Pray that every servant of the Word may bring the whole Gospel afresh to the church again and again, without twisting or changing anything whatsoever.

Lk. 12:48 Jesus clearly says that to whom much is given, of him much will be demanded. A servant of the Word must realize that more will be demanded of him than of others. There is no privilege in his task.

A leader of the church should certainly be admonished if someone feels he has done wrong. I remember how thankful I was years ago when a brother took me aside after a members' meeting – I had exploded at someone – and asked me, "Are you really sure your anger was of the Holy Spirit?" I had to admit that it was not, and so I called the meeting together again and

---

**Servant of the Word:* Pastor, minister; brother chosen by unanimous approval to serve his fellow members by caring for their inner and outer well-being. The term reflects the belief that authentic leadership in Christian community means service.

set it straight. If you feel that I or anyone is misusing his position of authority, please do me the favor of pointing it out.

We do not want a brotherhood that is bound to a man. I fear nothing more than a service in the church – whether teaching, counseling, or whatever – that binds someone emotionally to another person. It is terrible, and I want to have nothing to do with it. We must be bound together *in Christ.*

There is nothing I hate more than human beings having power over the souls and bodies of others, especially in Christian community. I have vowed to myself to fight this evil until the end of my life, and if anyone can point out to me where I have used power over a human being – even without my knowledge – I want to repent deeply for it. Personal power is the greatest enemy of a living church.

Mt. 18:2–4 Jesus put a child into his disciples' midst and said, "Unless you change and become like little children, you will never enter the kingdom of heaven. Therefore whoever humbles himself like this child is the greatest in the kingdom of heaven." Here we see that Jesus loves the childlike spirit. This should also be true among us. In a marriage, both husband and wife must want to be the least. And in church community, each member–whether elder or steward or whoever–must also want to be the least. That is our goal.

Speaking the truth, which is a task of a leader of the church, is not a gift given only to especially clever and superior men. If it were, most people would have reason to fear being a disciple of Jesus or a leader in the church. It is not man's intellect that is receptive to the truth; it is his childlike spirit. Jesus says, "Become
Mt. 18:3 like a child–only then will you be able to enter God's kingdom." The childlike spirit is and remains *spirit,* and because of that it is authority and revelation. The
Mt. 11:25 realization–that the truth is revealed only to children and to the simple-hearted–is crucial in the discipleship of Jesus.

From a letter: I was so thankful for your concern about our last members' meeting. So much was at stake, and yet we lost ourselves in trivial talk. The leadership I should have given as elder must have been lacking. There is always a tension: one does not want to dictate, but if everyone just talks as he pleases it is not good either, for then God's spirit cannot speak.

Someone who is given special responsibilities by the church – for example, a servant of the Word, housemother, steward, work distributor, or shop foreman – will either serve with humility or lord it over others as if they were his subjects. This is a danger for adults who work with children too. There is an inclination in each of us to want to be great. And even if it is a small inclination – perhaps someone tends to be a bit bossy – it is the beginning of a much greater evil that will in the end bring much suffering.

It is unbelievable what heartache can result when someone in a position of responsibility lets his authority be felt and treats his brothers and sisters as subjects. If a servant of the Word is bossy, it takes a certain courage to risk something and protest. But I wish all members that courage. No one but Jesus is our master, and we are all brothers.

Leaders of a church have no rights whatsoever over the souls entrusted to them. Consider how Jesus entrusted his flock to Peter. He did not give him any rights over the lambs. He only asked, "Do you love me?" And then he said, "Feed my sheep." It is a terrible sin – really nothing less than murder – when someone entrusted with a pastoral service thinks he has the right to govern souls. This also applies to those who care for children.

Jn. 21:15–17

I want nothing to do with human honor. I ask you never to honor a person, whoever he may be, but only
1 Cor. 3:1–15 Christ in him. We denounce the honoring of men, because it leads to sectarianism. In a sect the leader thinks he is great, but that is a horrible delusion. We want to honor Christ in our brothers and sisters; we want to love one another – Christ commanded us to. But we reject the idea of human greatness, which is foolishness before God.

We long deeply for all other powers and spirits to yield, and for our beloved Jesus to lay his pierced hands over each of us. We long for him to be with us all, and we long to be ready to serve him. We ask for everything superficial in us and everything that might hinder or frighten us to melt away. We want to acknowledge the rulership of Jesus alone. Yes, everything is in his hands: he is the ruler over all powers and principalities, the head of the church, and the vine of which we are only branches.

The revelation of Christ does not tolerate any human light next to it. If there is human light – pride and presumption – in any servant of the Word, it must be extinguished. Only the light of Jesus should rule in the church. God does not need human light. He needs men and women who wait in the darkness for his light, who hunger for truth and thirst for living water. If someone preaches the Gospel to his own credit and does not acknowledge that without God he can do nothing, he is a thief. He steals the words of Jesus and uses them for his own glory.

Jn. 15:4

Neither an individual nor a community can bear fruit without being united with Jesus. Once a person has decided to follow Jesus, he becomes a branch on the vine and cannot live for himself anymore. To separate and isolate oneself out of pride and self-glory is the way of the devil, and it ends in death. For every member of the church, but especially for its leaders, my wish is that they might dwell in Jesus, and still more, that Jesus might dwell in them.

Gifts

From a letter: Never forget that an act of love to one's fellowman is the only important act of the day. Everything else is of no value before God and may even tear us from him or separate us from our brothers.
Mt. 25:31–46 How strongly Jesus impresses this on our hearts in his prophecies about the last judgment! The question is never whether we are well-organized or act correctly, but whether we feed the hungry, take in strangers, clothe the naked, or visit those who are sick or in prison – in other words, whether we act out of love and compassion. Let us never pass by the need of another or forget the words and actions that strengthen love.

Just as no one has so few gifts that he cannot be moved by God, no one has so many gifts that he is too good to do simple manual work. We must be willing to do any service asked of us, to serve in the humblest place. A man may be the most gifted person in his community, but if he lacks humility, if his heart is not moved by the spirit of Jesus, his life will be unfruitful.

The parable of the talents is perhaps best understood
Mt. 25:14–30 in the context of the church: the talents are gifts given to different brothers and sisters. One person receives the gift of wisdom, another knowledge, another faith,

1 Cor. 12:8–10 healing, prophecy, discernment, speaking in tongues, or interpretation. These gifts are all required for the various tasks of the church, from leadership to any other. There is no difference in their importance; they all are parts of one body. The eye is no more important than the ear – they simply are two different organs.

Some people would like to see no differences. They think that if everyone were the same no one would know who was who, and then true justice would be established. But that is not the Gospel of Jesus. In Matthew 25, we read of a man who was given only one talent. This man felt he had not been given his fair share, and so he hated his master. He did nothing with his talent but hardened his heart. He not only lacked love, he was filled with hatred. He said, "Master, I knew you to be a hard man." That is the worst thing that can happen to us: to feel we have not been given our fair share; to feel that others have received more from God; and then to become so envious and loveless – so separated from the Body – that we do not contribute to it in any way at all. The master in the parable said, "You should have at least put the money in the bank." He meant, "Do at least the little you are able to do."

Mt. 25:24–30

One person is brilliant, another deft with his hands, another very musical. These are natural gifts, and they should not be buried, though for the common good of the church they often have to be sacrificed. It would be wrong if someone with intellectual gifts thought he could do only intellectual work–otherwise he would

Mt. 25:18

be "burying his talents"–or if a very musical person thought she was wasting her talent by doing menial work. We must be willing to sacrifice our natural talents for the sake of the whole Body.

From a letter: You write that you are not very gifted. That does not matter. No one has so few gifts that he

1 Pt. 4:8–11

cannot be moved by God. What matters is that you use the gifts you *do* possess–that they are brought into movement by God. It is never a lack of gifts that is the problem, but a lack of readiness to be used by God.

1 Cor. 12–13

In 1 Corinthians 12 and 13, the apostle Paul speaks of many different gifts, including prophecy, leadership, healing, and speaking in tongues. But then he says that all these great gifts are nothing without love. Our communal life is a gift too, but unless God gives us love over and over again, it will become as lifeless as a machine.

The gift of discernment of spirits is vital for a living church, but it must be given by God. It is not a human gift. When we as individuals or a group tolerate a mixture of spirits in our midst, we lose contact with the spirit of God, even if we think we are being broad-minded.

On the other hand, we must guard against fighting impure or false spirits with human zeal and correcting or criticizing one another out of fear that something false might enter the church. We must recognize the importance of discerning spirits, yet we must also recognize that it is no help to separate them in a human way.

Mt. 13:24–30

The parable of the wheat and weeds growing together in one field shows how we can cause harm by attempting to "clean the field" ourselves. The disciples were full of zeal, but Jesus warned them to be careful, saying, "Wait, lest in gathering the weeds you root up the wheat along with them." There is always the danger of correcting too much, of admonishing each other too much. The only answer is for us to be more dependent on God.

Acts 2:4

The gift of speaking in tongues was granted at Pentecost through the outpouring of the Holy Spirit. It was definitely a divine and holy experience, and we should have deep reverence for it. I believe that today, too, such holy experiences may be given. But we must guard against the spirit of error.

People speak too lightly about being "filled with the Spirit" and possessing "gifts of the Spirit." These terms are often applied to speaking in tongues, but in the New Testament these phrases are used in that

connection only in a few instances. In many other
instances there is no mention of tongues. Who would
dare to say that one cannot be filled with the Holy
Spirit without the evidence of tongues? Thirty years
Lk. 1:41,67 before Pentecost, Elizabeth and Zechariah were "filled
with the Holy Spirit." And there have been millions of
instances since then when people who did not speak in
tongues were brought to salvation.

In the early church, speaking in tongues was closely
related to repentance. Jesus started his mission with
a call to repentance, and the apostle Peter, too, began
Acts 2:38 his mission with the words, "Repent and be baptized
for the forgiveness of your sins." If we have not
honestly repented and believed in Jesus Christ, then
we have not received the Holy Spirit. Unfortunately,
there is a lack of repentance in many of today's
movements which see speaking in tongues as being
"filled with the Spirit."

It is unwise to equate the receiving of the Holy Spirit with the pouring-out of particular emotions. As if that were the only way the Spirit worked! His indwelling does not depend on our emotions, but on our union with Christ, which is accomplished by God through our faith in him. The biblical conditions for receiving the Holy Spirit are repentance, faith in Christ, and the remission or forgiveness of our sins.

Acts 2
1 Cor. 12
1 Cor. 13

From a letter: We must have reverence for the gift of speaking in tongues as described in Acts 2 and 1 Corinthians 12. But it is false and unhealthy to make a teaching or religion out of such a gift. In 1 Corinthians 13 we are told to ask for the higher gifts of faith, hope, and love, of which the greatest is love.

Mt. 6:6

The gift of love leads to Jesus Christ, to community, to outreach, and to mission; it does not lead to talking about our own spiritual gifts. If we are filled with love, we may well speak in tongues, but we need not talk about it. Jesus says, "Go into your room, lock the door, and pray to God in heaven. Then your Father, who sees what is done in secret, will reward you."

The charismatic movement, which lays so much emphasis on speaking in tongues, is based on false teachings that bring division; it brings honor and glory to men rather than to God. If someone came to me and said he could speak in tongues, I would advise him not to talk about it but rather to show the fruits of the Spirit as described in the Sermon on the Mount. Jesus did not teach us to speak in tongues but to refrain from making a show of our religion and to go the way of humility, love, and unity.

It is not the development of man that will change the course of human history–only the intervention of the living God in men's lives. When he has touched us, we may hope for a change of heart and soul and for the Spirit and the kingdom of God to come. The Spirit brings the joy of God: joy in love, joy in sharing with brothers and sisters, joy in pure relationships between men and women, and joy in justice and peace among races and nations. Of ourselves we remain poor, helpless, and tormented. But we must believe that the joy of God and his kingdom can change earth and heaven!

Forgiveness

It should be quite out of the question for anyone to come to prayer without having forgiven his brother, his neighbor, or even his enemy. Jesus clearly says,
Mt. 6:14–15 "He who does not forgive will not be forgiven." We cannot change one iota of this truth. The only way to find inner peace in Christ is through peace with one's brothers. Unforgiving thoughts lead to separation, and separation brings inner harm and leads to death. Complete peace demands complete honesty. We can live in peace with our brothers only if we carry the truth in our hearts and are honest in our love.

From a letter: True forgiveness of sins is possible only
Eph. 1:7 in Jesus. In the world people forgive one another's
Col. 1:14 sins, but without Jesus, which is no help. At the time of the Reformation, the Catholic Church, which had tremendous influence over people, "forgave" sins through the sale of indulgences. Today, psychologists and psychiatrists "forgive" sin. They tell people, "You have not sinned; your behavior is quite normal; there is nothing wrong with it. You don't need to have a bad conscience; you can't help it." That is how the world forgives sin.

Things go wrong in churches and Christian communities because Jesus' words about making peace with one another before bringing a gift to the altar are not taken seriously anymore. Jesus himself said this, and as his followers we are entrusted with witnessing to his words. To us this means we should not come to prayer or partake of the Lord's Supper unless there is complete peace among us. Too often it happens that things are left unresolved when people pray together. But communal life will not endure like that, and neither will marriage. We must clear things up and forgive one another again and again.

Mt. 5:23–24

If we hold a grudge against someone, the door to God will be closed. It will be absolutely closed, with no way to him. Only if we forgive others will we be forgiven. I am sure that many prayers are not heard because the person praying has a grudge against someone, even if he is not aware of it. Jesus says more than once that before we pray we must forgive. If we want Jesus, we must have a forgiving heart.

Mt. 6:14–15

Just as it did in the time of the apostles, the church of Jesus Christ has the authority to represent his kingdom today. It has the authority to loose and to bind, to forgive and to leave unforgiven. Without the forgiveness of sin no conscience can live, and without it no

Mt. 18:18

Mt. 6:14–15 one can enter the kingdom of God. But unless we first forgive others, we cannot receive forgiveness.

Jas. 5:16 In the Letter of James we read that we should confess our sins to one another so that they may be forgiven. But this is possible only if Jesus lives in us. Without him there is no forgiveness.

Unless forgiveness of sins is spoken out in communion with Jesus, through his Holy Spirit, it means nothing. It is Jesus who promises that he will forgive us at the last judgment, and it is he who will also overcome demons and devils on that day. We ourselves cannot overcome evil, even if we live together in brotherhood, even if we are burned as martyrs. Unless Jesus lives in us and we in him, our efforts are all in vain.

Rv. 1:5–6 The words "To him who loves us and has freed us from our sins…be glory and power for ever and ever" indicate that it is not we who can forgive sins. Forgiveness of sins is possible only through Christ, who loves us and frees us with his life's blood.

We pronounce forgiveness of sins in the united church, yet this forgiveness descends from heaven – we ourselves have no authority whatsoever. Nothing human can take over. The grace of the cross must be present.

As a burning candle consumes itself and gives light, so the light of the risen Christ shines out to us through his death. When Christ arises in us – when the sun comes up – night is overcome by day. So it is with the forgiveness of sins. We must experience what it means to be burdened with sin *and then freed.* Then we will see how the sun of Christ shines anew through the forgiveness of sins.

The redeeming power of forgiveness, which is in Jesus alone, must remain the center of the living church and of our expectation for the whole world.

Forgiveness means personal redemption and freeing, but it must always be seen in the greater context of redemption for the whole world. We should expect it to bring the kingdom of peace to whole nations and to all men. This expectation, which can be found on every page of the New Testament, is from Jesus. It must be alive in us so that it is not just something we believe in but something that burns in our hearts.

Because Jesus died for us, his blood speaks louder than the blood of Abel, who symbolizes the innocent man who has been slain. In Jesus even a murderer can find forgiveness. The blood of Jesus speaks louder than the accusing blood shed by the hand of man.

Mt. 6:14–15 We have Christ's wonderful promise that if we forgive we will be forgiven. Certainly we also have his sharp warning that if we do not forgive we will not be forgiven. Let us look at one another with new eyes and see each other as a gift from God, even if we know each other's weaknesses.

Col. 3:15 Paul writes to the Colossians that they are called to live in the peace of Christ as members of one body. It is not enough to feel the peace of God around us – it should reign in our hearts. The soul of man groans for peace. Therefore Jesus said to his disciples on his last
Jn. 14:27 evening, "I give you my peace. It is not peace such as the world gives."

By nature we are not at peace; we are divided. But we are called to find reconciliation with God in Jesus. He offers us forgiveness of sins so that we may find unity and peace with him and with one another. It is not enough to seek peace for ourselves, for our own souls. We must seek it for the whole Body and ultimately for the whole creation.

Resentment

From a letter: Every serious Christian must go through hours of godforsakenness; even Jesus himself did. The
Lk. 23:46 only answer in such hours is: "Father, into thy hands I commit my spirit." If we give ourselves unconditionally to the Father, he will show us the way. But nothing will be shown to him who does not forgive his brother.

God will not have mercy on him, and he will remain godforsaken as long as he continues in his hatred and unforgiveness.

From a letter: Be firm in your rejection of all touchiness and anything else that destroys love. Beloved brother and sister, you are not the only ones who could find reason to be touchy. I am hated and accused by many; yet if I gave in to resentment, the door of prayer to God would be closed to me. God hears only those who forgive.

From a letter: I feel pained that at your young age you have to undergo such difficult struggles. But do not blame your troubles on your father. Through Adam we are all under the curse of sin and death and cannot find new life or purity of heart except through the blood of Christ. That is the same for you as for me and for any other human being. Hold on to Jesus.

Rom. 5:12–21

From a letter: You are cynical about the deception that has been revealed among us. Yes, it is terrible – so terrible that it could tear one completely apart. But you are only adding sin to sin if you become bitter. Read Psalm 22; consider what happened to Jesus and how he reacted to mockery, contempt, and betrayal. It did not make him cynical.

Ps. 22

From a letter: You ask for forgiveness for your envy and hatred. We personally will gladly forgive you. But the forgiveness of the whole brotherhood, which means the renewal of unity with Jesus and his church, cannot be given until you turn fully away from your sin.

We are not angry with you, but we cannot pronounce forgiveness on behalf of the brotherhood for your sinful attitude until you prove your repentance more deeply. This may have already begun. If so, continue in that direction. God is good, and he will not reject you. The brotherhood loves you, too, and will not reject you either. But we cannot unite with you as long as there is envy and hatred in you.

From a letter: You wrote that it was impossible for you to work because you were so upset about the hurt done to you. Your resentment must come to light and be overcome. Ultimately, the wrongs other people have done to you cannot separate you from God; only the wrongs you do to others. This is of utmost importance: all hurt and bitterness must be overcome.

From a letter: Hold firm to hope and faith, and deep joy will fill your heart and heal your wounds – joy that will overcome all fear and pessimism. After all, we are called to a way of joy – joy in God and in one another, for in the deepest sense love means joy.

Unity

Mt. 23:37 In Matthew 23:37 Jesus says, "How often have I wanted to gather you to me as a hen gathers her chicks, and you would not." This plea, along with the
Jn. 17:21 plea in Jesus' last prayer–"May they all be one, Father, even as I am one with thee"–is a decisive and constant challenge to us. It calls us to a way of complete brotherly love and oneness in Jesus, and it calls us to follow him in unity so that the world may recognize we are his disciples.

Nothing binds or unites people more deeply than having the same hope, the same faith, the same joy and expectation. It is very sad, therefore, when individual believers stand alone. There have always been people who had to stand alone on account of their faith–some of them in prison, for years. But where there is true expectation, people are usually drawn together; their common faith leads to community, and they can strengthen and encourage one another. Standing for God always has a unifying power. Let us pray that we may be gathered together with all those who live in expectation of him.

Mt. 22:37–39 *From a letter:* Jesus' first commandment is to love God with all our heart, soul, and being, and then to love our neighbor as ourselves. In this individualistic

age more than ever, a church of people committed to one another in such love and faithfulness is an absolute necessity. Jesus stresses the importance of love and absolute unity – unity such as he has with the Father – again and again. I do not think we have ever reached this ultimate state of unity, even in our holiest moments; only God knows. Yet we want to live as a
1 Jn. 4:19–21 witness to it. We cannot separate dedication to Jesus from dedication to our brothers and sisters.

From a letter: It is true that Jesus can be served anywhere. But what a special gift it is when through him two or three or more people become of one heart and one soul! This cannot be manufactured; it is a gift.

God does not contradict himself. He does not say to one, "Thou shalt go to war," and to another, "Thou shalt not go to war"; or to one, "Thou shalt be faithful in marriage," and to the other, "Thou art free to divorce." If we are open to the truth – if we listen to God in our hearts – we will find that he says the same thing to all, also in practical matters. We do not believe
1 Cor. 1:10 in the rule of a majority over a minority. We believe in the unanimity brought about by Christ, who wants to speak the same truth in every heart. This unity is a grace and a miracle we experience again and again. But if we are unfaithful to God and to each other, it can be taken from us.

The unity of all believers is the only criterion for truth. When true unity is lacking, charisma – the power of individual persons or personalities over others – takes its place. People listen in a human way to others merely because they are strong personalities or leaders. Charisma is not only the wrong foundation for community; it is altogether dangerous ground.

A religious group can find a healthy inner life only if its members find unity again and again with the Spirit and with God. Only then can the conscience of each one live and thrive, and only then can true unanimity be achieved.

It is immaterial where unity is lived. The important thing is that it *is* lived somewhere.

Many people today seek religious experiences or charismatic gifts like speaking in tongues. But there is a danger that in seeking these gifts people miss the main message of the Gospel: unity in love. What help would it be to humankind if thousands and tens of thousands of people spoke in tongues but had no love and unity?

Our faith in Jesus Christ unites us as brothers and sisters and urges us to call others to follow him with us. We do this in absolute poverty of spirit – it is not that we want to make more members. But we do feel urged to call others to unity. The Holy Spirit does not scatter; it unites.

Mt. 12:30

The attempt to reconcile different churches and confessions is without any doubt good. But true unity – the unity that breaks down all barriers – starts with repentance. When the Holy Spirit came down at Pentecost, people asked, "Brothers, what shall we do?" They were deeply struck in their hearts, and they repented for their sins and became of one heart and one soul. Unfortunately, in today's ecumenical movement barriers or fences often remain, and people shake hands over them. But we must testify to the possibility of true unity among men. It comes only through repentance and through personally facing Jesus – as man, as living spirit, and as Lord.

Acts 2:37

From a letter: The ecumenical movement tends to resolve differences by making concessions. Concessions take the place of repentance, deep reconciliation, and the unanimity that grows as the fruit of repentance, and in the end serious evils are often smeared over.

A merely emotional feeling of unity is not enough. In our communities we promise to speak openly to one another when there are problems – to admonish each other and to accept admonition. Whenever we avoid this brotherly honesty because we fear the consequences it might have, our unity is no longer a reality. God's will is deed, and we must live according to it with deeds. When we do this, Christ can bring about a truly united church, purified by the Holy Spirit. We will no longer nurse feelings against others, and we will become of one heart and one soul, as in the early Church.

Mt. 12:33 Jesus said more than once that a tree is recognized
Mt. 7:16–18 by its fruits. We must never forget this. All of us can see what kind of tree today's society is: its fruits are murder, injustice, impurity, unfaithfulness, and destruction.

What were the fruits Jesus wanted to see? The first fruit is unity. How else shall the world recognize his
Jn. 17:21 disciples? Jesus said, "May they all be one, Father, even as we are one."

How can we show the fruits of unity and remain a part of today's society? It is impossible: society is ruled by mammon, the spirit of this world, which is "a liar
Jn. 8:44 and a murderer from the beginning." It is ruled not by the spirit of unity but by the spirits of disintegration, destruction, and separation. True unity can be found only in a life of brotherhood.

Is it not true that Christ demands the surrender of the *whole* man to his new order? The time is urgent. Let us come to a true sense of responsibility! Let us gather with Christ and unite with him as branches on the tree of life!

In a brotherhood ruled by the Holy Spirit one can see many aspects of Jesus, just as one sees different colors in a rainbow. Each of us is different, but God created us, and we should not try to be something that we are not. We should give our heart, soul, and being to Jesus and let him do with us what he wants. Then our lives will find true fulfillment, and we will love each other as we are, with our differences – even our national differences. The same Jesus is expressed in every brother and sister.

Church Discipline

In our church communities each member makes a covenant with God at baptism and promises never again to sin willfully against him. If after baptism someone does sin willfully against God, he must undergo church discipline in order to make a completely new beginning.

The small sins we all commit every day can be forgiven through our daily prayer. If the sins are worse, they can be forgiven through confession. James says, "Confess your sins to one another, and pray for one another, and then you will be healed." For more serious sins, church discipline is necessary.

Jas. 5:16

Discipline is carried out only at the request of the person concerned. In some cases a person may be excluded from common prayer and from members' meetings until he has repented and is forgiven. In others, a person is put into the "small exclusion." This means that he may not take part in common prayer and should not be given the greeting of peace, though he may still participate in the daily life of the community. If an even graver sin is committed, the church may use the "great exclusion." In this case, a person is pronounced cut off from the kingdom of

---

*For the biblical basis of church discipline as described in this chapter, see Mt. 5:29–30, 9:13, 16:19, 18:8–9, 15–20; Lk. 15:7–10; Jn. 20:22–23; 1 Cor. 5:1–5; 1 Tm. 1:20.

God, and he may take no part in the communal life of the church until he has found a repentant heart.

When someone has to repent of an especially dark, willfully committed sin, we use Paul's words, "I give

1 Cor. 5:1–5

you over to Satan for the destruction of your flesh and the salvation of your soul." Paul was speaking of a man who lived with his father's wife, yet even after such a sin he believed that exclusion could lead to the salvation of this man's soul. We also believe – and have experienced it – that through discipline people who have sinned can find full repentance and full forgiveness and can become true brothers and sisters again.

Heb. 12:15

Paul warned the early church to let no bitter weed grow up to poison the whole. If this warning was given to the earliest believers, then it surely applies to us too. That is one reason we use church discipline: so that no poison may destroy the church. Another reason is to give the person who is disciplined a chance to begin anew, to find forgiveness of sins, and to purify his or her life.

We can exclude a brother or sister only if we recognize that the sin in our own hearts must be judged as well. Church discipline is not carried out to judge a person, but to separate the evil in a person from the church. This has to happen again and again in our own hearts.

When brothers and sisters accept church discipline, it should remind us of the grace of repentance. If they really repent, they do something for the whole church–in fact, for the whole world–because evil is overcome by Jesus. In this sense we must have deep respect and reverence for those who are disciplined, because we know that we need God's mercy and compassion ourselves.

We must be very careful not to load onto a person even one milligram more than his actual guilt. We should be thankful that repentance and reconciliation with God is possible for those excluded, for us, and for all humankind.

Church discipline is a victory of light over darkness; it is the beginning of healing in a person. If it is accepted in this sense–the only true sense–it is a grace.

I believe that the question of exclusion and reacceptance–as indeed of church discipline altogether–is closely connected with Jesus, the loving and redeeming Savior who bears the sins of the whole world. He accepted death on the cross so that all men would be given the possibility of finding reconciliation with God again and again. This reconciliation cannot be separated from the forgiveness of sins.

The whole question of church discipline is something that has become blurred or softened in Christendom today. But it is not a matter of our church's point of view versus the view of Christianity in

general. Our understanding of church discipline is
Mt. 18:15–20 based wholly on the words of Jesus and his apostles. They are our only guide.

In a church that is almost dead or totally dead, people gossip about one another's weaknesses. There is little, if any, church discipline, and therefore no forgiveness either. Jesus commanded, "When you go to the altar
Mt. 5:23–24 to bring your sacrifice and you remember that your brother has something against you, go back and make peace with him, and then bring your sacrifice to the altar." He also said that we should not pray unless
Mk. 11:25 we forgive *every* person in the whole world, whether the person is right or wrong, friend or enemy. These commands have been almost entirely forgotten.

Mt. 13:24–30 Jesus' parable about the weeds among the wheat is often used as an excuse for a dying church. But I believe that this parable is not chiefly meant for the church; it is meant mainly for the world in general. We cannot use it as an excuse for tolerating evil. If we know there is sin in the church, it must be rooted out through church discipline, out of love to the person involved and to the church. Otherwise the whole church will be lost. Paul says that the church should
Eph. 5:27 not have spots, blemishes, or wrinkles, but be pure and
Col. 1:22 holy as Jesus himself is holy. We cannot excuse evil by saying that where there is wheat there is always chaff.

There is no better way to defeat the devil in our own hearts than by giving ourselves completely to Jesus. This is especially true for members under church discipline and for those who struggle with evil thoughts and feelings. They must give themselves over to Jesus again and again. That is the only way victory is possible in the struggle of the heart in daily life.

Heb. 4:12

In the Letter to the Hebrews it says that the word of God is as sharp as a two-edged sword. We should apply this sharpness to ourselves first of all. But the New Testament also speaks of the great compassion, love, and warmth that come from the Spirit, and we should always show this love to others, especially to sinners.

We can come to Jesus with any need, and we will find compassion and grace. But we must be willing to accept his sharpness, too. Every Christian needs someone who speaks the truth to him in the love of Christ, no matter how painful it is, in order to cut through what is evil in him.

We must pray that along with the salt of the truth we may have compassion and merciful love. Then we will not fall into extremes, and we will not speak to each other without love. My father once wrote, "He who admonishes his brother without love is a murderer." I think all of us have to recognize where we have been loveless, and ask for forgiveness.*

When something is not right in a brother or sister, we must speak to him or her about it out of love. And if someone speaks plainly to us, we must not be touchy. I can assure you that those who lived with Jesus heard plenty of straight talking. In comparison to Jesus, we are perhaps still much too polite. Jesus honored his
Jn. 2:4 mother, but he also said to her, "What have I to do with you, woman?" His way of love is not a way of politeness.

From a letter: If you know of specific instances of complacency, lovelessness, or sin among us, please bring them to our attention. But don't make general accusations and talk about them with others. Such talking is extremely dangerous and divisive. It will not help to bring brothers and sisters together but will drive them further apart.

It is very clear from the New Testament that forgiveness of sin is connected with the church. Jesus gives

---

*Another similar saying of Eberhard Arnold is "Love without truth lies, but truth without love kills."

Mt. 16:19 the keys "to bind and to loose" to the church. So anywhere on this earth where two or three meet in his name – that is, in a spirit of total and unconditional surrender to him – there the keys to bind and to loose are given. Forgiveness is not merely a private matter.

God wants us to become clearer in discernment, but he also wants us to become more loving, more understanding, and more merciful. Church discipline must exist, but we must remember Jesus' words, "He who
Lk. 6:37–38 judges will be judged" and "With the same measure you use, you will be measured." Love is the greatest gift.

Baptism

In baptism three things are of utmost importance: faith in Jesus Christ, assurance of the forgiveness of sins through repentance, and incorporation into the Body, which is the church.

Baptism is a covenant with God and his church in which we give ourselves wholeheartedly to Jesus with all that we are and have, in the belief that he will forgive our sins. This forgiveness of sins is possible only
Eph. 1:7 through the death of Jesus, though he has given his
Jn. 20:23 church the power to forgive sins in his name.

May God forgive the sins of each person who desires baptism, and may Jesus purify each of them
1 Jn. 1:7 with his blood and make them children of God and true brothers and sisters.

Baptism is a confession of repentance, and therefore it means absolute dedication: it means giving ourselves, pouring ourselves out totally for Jesus Christ, as a vessel is poured out, so that we become empty of ourselves and poor before God.

1 Pt. 3:21 Baptism is the declaration of a good conscience before God, which is possible only through the gracious help

Rom. 6:3–6 and cleansing power of Christ's blood. It is Christ's Jn. 15:26 spirit, the spirit of truth, that speaks to the believing conscience and directs it toward unity with the will of God. Only in such unity – the unity of a good conscience with God – is there true peace. Here the Rom. 7:6 conscience is freed from the law and from the powers of the spirit of our time.

Jesus was baptized in the Jordan River, and I believe he meant baptism to be a real immersion. But the form is not important – if there is no water available for immersion, water can also be poured over the Col. 2:12 person being baptized. The important thing is that we are buried with Christ in baptism and raised with him through the faith which God works in us, just as Christ was raised from the dead.

The step of baptism is a step of total dedication to God and the church, and we do not want to persuade anyone to take it. But we must call people to repentance; we must point out that the Gospel contains the sharpest condemnation of sin, though it also contains the warmest welcome for repentant sinners. God calls us again and again to come to him with our trespasses and our need, and we can always turn trustingly to him, no matter what the circumstances.

From a letter: We do not become better people through baptism; we do not climb up to become gods. We will always remain lowly sinners to whom God comes down. It is a miracle we are never worthy of, yet God is full of grace.

It is better to remain unbaptized than to take the step half-heartedly for the sake of parents or someone you love, or in order to find security in church membership. Baptism must be a personal decision. No one can make it for you.

Millions of people are baptized, but for many of them baptism is a completely dead form. I would advise anyone who wants to be baptized to ask himself, Lk. 14:25–27 "Am I willing, for the sake of Jesus, to love nothing more than him – neither wife, parents, nor children – so that he can live in me? Am I willing to give every thing to Jesus and my brothers?" If you are not, don't be baptized. You must be willing to die for him so that he himself may live in your heart. Jesus must be your only treasure.

If you are baptized for the sake of Jesus, he will receive Rom. 8:1–4 you and love you and give you his forgiveness and peace. He will live within you, and help you conquer every temptation. You will be purified and washed clean by his blood.

Rom. 6:3–6
True baptism is deeply related to the death and the resurrection of Jesus. It cannot be separated from
Jn. 12:24–25
them. Baptism really means dying with Christ and then rising with him. The phrase "dying with Christ" has been so overused that perhaps some of its power has been lost; but when we consider deeply what it meant for God to come to this earth and die for us, we will begin to feel the seriousness of his asking us to die with him.

Baptism requires a personal decision to confess one's sins and to give one's life to Jesus completely. It means wanting to die rather than consciously sin again. You must personally experience that Christ is your peace of heart and that he died for you. But this is not enough. You must have a much greater vision of Christ. It would be wrong to forget your personal experience, yet you must see beyond it and recognize the greatness of the suffering and sin of the whole world. And you must also recognize the greatness of God, the greatness of the universe, and the greatness of Jesus, who is king
Rv. 1:18
over the kingdom of God and holds the key to the underworld. He has power over all powers.

Baptism is not a human institution: it is a step in which sins are forgiven and demons are driven out through Jesus Christ and the Holy Spirit. No man can do this, nor can any group of people. We need

the presence of Christ himself, and therefore we ask for God to be present at our baptismal meetings. It is he whom we honor, he who forgives our sins through faith in the death of Jesus Christ. Of course, before God can forgive sins through baptism, there must be repentance. All of us must take repentance seriously, and all of us must break with human justice, human goodness, and human fairness. No one of us is right; God alone is right. Jesus was sharpest to those who were "good"–to those who did not need the cross or believed that since they were Abraham's children they
Mk. 2:17 were saved. He said, "It is not the healthy who need a physician, but the sick. I have come not to save virtuous people, but sinners."

Rom. 6:12–13 Paul says that once we are converted and baptized–once we have decided to follow Jesus–we should no longer put the members of our body at the disposal of sin. This is very important: the brain must be filled by God's grace and God's thoughts; the hands must no longer cause the shedding of blood or carry out impure or obscene acts; and the eyes must no longer be used for lust, but to radiate God's love to brothers and sisters. When we give ourselves to Christ in baptism, we seal our whole body for his use.

Yet everyone knows that after baptism, evil still tries to work in us. In one it may be through impurity, in another it may be through pride, in another through hatred and bitterness. It is impossible to pull ourselves out of the mud by our own shoe-strings. We may fight and struggle, but we will never be able to change ourselves. It is through the death of Jesus, his forgiveness, and his power to drive out evil from the heart

1 Cor. 10:13 that we will no longer be slaves to sin. We will still be tempted, but our temptation will be answered by the deep inner experience of faith. If we have only the law–the "thou shalt not desire"–and evil desire comes up in our hearts, we won't know what to do with it. But if we have experienced Jesus through repentance, we will be able to overcome. We will still be human, but we will no longer be slaves to sin.

The Lord's Supper

The Lord's Supper is an outward symbol, a sign of giving ourselves in brokenness to Jesus, whose body was broken and crucified. Christ wants to be present in the heart of each one who breaks the bread and drinks the wine. He wants us to become weak with him so that we may then become strong in his strength and have communion with him. Bread and wine are only symbols, but the purifying unity with Christ which they symbolize is a great reality. At the Lord's Supper we experience community with Christ.

1 Cor. 10:16–17 Just as grains of wheat from different fields are ground and formed into one loaf, and grapes from many vineyards are pressed to produce wine, so we, who come from different countries and cultures, can be united in the Lord's Supper. But this unity is possible only when we sacrifice our self-importance.

The Lord's Supper is a meal of unity, and we should prepare ourselves so that we may partake of it in the right way. It is a meal at which we remember Jesus, whose redeeming spirit of forgiveness is there for the whole world – for all people and all races. And it is also a time for us to renew our covenant of faithfulness to God and unburden our hearts so that they may be freed for service and rededicated to him.

As we remember how Jesus appointed the meal on his last evening on earth, we should also remember that every Christian should be ready to sacrifice his life – in fact *should* sacrifice his life – like him. We live in a world that is just as hostile to God's kingdom as it was in Jesus' time, and he did not promise us that we would fare better than he did. Rather, he said that his

Jn. 15:18–20 disciples would be persecuted and that what was done to their master would be done to them too.

By celebrating the Lord's Supper we testify to the love of our Lord Jesus, whose death made it possible for us to find forgiveness of sins, love, and unity with one another. It is actually a very simple meal, but Jesus asked his disciples to hold it in memory of him, and so we celebrate it in that sense.

1 Cor. 11:29 Paul says that he who eats the bread and drinks the wine unworthily at the Meal of Remembrance eats and drinks judgment on himself. It is clear by this that we should not go to the Lord's Supper with a conscience burdened by unconfessed sin. But we should not allow feelings of unworthiness to torment us. Paul is speaking here mainly about the inner attitude with which we should come to the Lord's Supper. We should come with the same reverent fear Moses had

when God showed him the burning bush and said to
Ex. 3:5 him, "Take off your shoes, here is holy ground."

In the early church the believers met often to hold the Lord's Supper so that evil spirits would be driven out from among them. When a spiritual struggle is going on in our brotherhood, we, too, feel urged to celebrate the Lord's Supper. Jörg Blaurock, an early Anabaptist leader, said that if it is celebrated often, it will reveal any false brothers among us.

In the breaking of bread and drinking of wine at the Lord's Supper, we join ourselves to Christ in the deepest sense possible. We remember his saving
1 Cor. 11:26 death and "proclaim it until he comes," as Paul says. We proclaim Christ's death as the greatest historical event: through his wounds we are healed, through his suffering we find God, and through his great light we find love. We pray that he alone may be our Lord and master. Let us love him–his way and his life–with all our being.

Mt. 10:39 The New Testament says that if we love Christ, we must die with him. This means we must die to ourselves. Dying to oneself is often very painful and may cost a long struggle, but it is possible if we love Christ and his cross deeply enough. It is not a matter of self-torment but of finding Jesus.

Certainly we should not only remember Christ's death and his suffering when we think of the Lord's Supper—we should also remember his resurrection from the dead and his ascension to the Father, from whose side he will rule the church and the heart of every believer. And we should remember his promise to come again to judge us and to establish his wonderful kingdom.

Love and Marriage

Love

Jesus showed us that love means giving one's life for others rather than taking life, becoming the lowest and humblest rather than the most powerful. Love makes us free. A person who wants to dominate others and have power over them has a tormented soul, whereas a person who is burning with love has a joyful soul. We wish for our couples that love might rule their lives, and that service to one another might come before service to oneself. But more than this, we wish that they might be dedicated to the great cause of God, and that their love to him might come before everything else – even before their marriage.

In the sphere of love, the determining factor is always the nonphysical: it is the relationship from heart to heart and from soul to soul. We cannot forget that without the soul, the body is merely the human form – merely matter. Yet we should not despise it on that account. "Do you not know that your body is a shrine of the indwelling Holy Spirit, and the Spirit is God's gift to you?" The body gives expression to the impulses of the heart. A gentle smile, eyes that shine

1 Cor. 6:19

*For this chapter extensive use has been made of the author's book *In the Image of God: Marriage and Chastity in Christian Life* (Plough, 1977).

from an affectionate word, or a tender touch of the hand can lead to an ardent embrace and caresses of final fulfillment in union. The body is the soul made visible.

From a letter: The attraction to the opposite sex is natural, but it is not sufficient ground by far on which to marry or found a family. It is quite natural that when a man loves a woman, he wants to know if she is the "right" one. There is only one answer to this question: both must feel that a marital relationship will lead them nearer to Jesus.

I can well imagine – in actual fact, I know it for sure – that the right choice for a spouse is not the one who is most attractive erotically, but the one whose companionship will lead both partners closer to Jesus. If marriage is based only on physical attraction, it will go to pieces easily.

From a letter: In considering a partner for life, do not let your feelings of affection move casually from one person to another. Test your feelings before Jesus. The step of marriage is right for a Christian only if he is assured that it will lead him closer to Jesus, and that both partners will serve Jesus more fully together than alone. I do not believe that a Christian should get married purely to satisfy his physical and emotional desires. A personal, emotional desire needs to be there, but it should not be the decisive factor.

From a letter: If you are thinking of binding another soul to your life through marriage, learn to love, learn to be open-hearted, and learn to consider the other person first.

From a letter: I mean it seriously and for your well-being: it is better to be sure now – before you make any commitment to each other – whether or not it is God's will that you two belong together. To have doubts once you have committed yourself through an engagement is terrible, but to have doubts once you are married is unbelievably more terrible. May God make it clear to you whether or not you really belong together. It would be better to have a shocking end to your relationship than a shock without end. I say this to you out of love. May God lead you.

From a letter: Your question "Why do I feel attracted toward this boy if he is not meant for me but for someone else?" is a bit of a rebellious one. It accuses someone higher than yourself. Ultimately it accuses God. Human nature being what it is, we often feel attractions that we have no choice but to reject. That is simply part of our human weakness. Who is destined for you, or whether or not someone is destined for you, is not for me to say. The important thing for you is to give your life to Jesus.

Marriage

Mt. 5:28

Jesus takes the bond of marriage so seriously that he calls even a lustful glance "adultery in the heart." He speaks so sharply about this because he wants to protect the wonderful and holy gift of unity between two people.

In a true marriage a man and a woman become one first of all in spirit. This means that they are one in faith, one in their experience of God, and united in the purity of the church.

Second, marriage means that a man and a woman are one in soul. One can be of one spirit with any believing person. But there is a difference in the bond that exists between a married couple and between others. There is a special love between these two, and a special joy when they are near to one another. Because they love one another quite specifically, they are faithful to one another and keep their relationship pure.

Third, marriage means that a couple becomes one flesh through the act of physical union. If this union is broken by unfaithfulness, it is a terrible sin, because–in God's eyes–everything in the marriage is smashed. What was first a blessing becomes a curse, and nothing is left except the hope that through repentance and God's grace something new can be given again. There is no excuse for adultery, especially not for anyone who believes in Jesus.

The blessing of God is on any couple – young or old – who experiences unity in the right order: first unity of one spirit, then oneness of heart and soul, and then physical union. Too often a couple becomes one in body when there is little oneness of heart and only very little oneness of spirit.

Mt. 5:27–32 We take Jesus' words in the Sermon on the Mount about lust, divorce, and remarriage very seriously and maintain a sharp stand against sexual immorality. No member of our church may divorce and then remarry, and no remarried person may become a committed member while continuing to live in such a marriage relationship if a former spouse is still living.

We believe in life-long faithfulness, also for the sake of any children there may be. The covenant of marriage between two people must be a covenant for life, and it cannot be tampered with: "What God has
Mt. 19:6 joined together, let no man put asunder."

The basis of a true marriage is love to Jesus. You must accept Jesus as a living power into your relationship. You must surrender completely to him.

Eph. 5:23 It is the task of the man to represent Jesus as the head, but this also means that he must follow Jesus' example of lowliness. A man who does not want to be lowly cannot be a disciple.

The task of the woman is to represent Jesus as the Body, the church. She must take the example of Mary,
Lk. 1:38 who said, "Here am I, the lowly handmaiden of the Lord." If she cannot accept this, she is not a Christian.

In the deepest sense, marriage leads to community. As
Gn. 2:18 God said, "It is not good for man to be alone." Out of one being he made two – man and woman – and in marriage these two become one again.

A marriage will last only if both partners have humble and open hearts. Jealousy and self-importance will always try to enter their relationship and separate them, but love will overcome, because it is "neither
1 Cor. 13:4–7 arrogant nor rude. It does not insist on its own way; it is not irritable or resentful; it does not rejoice at wrong, but rejoices in the truth." This also means that love forgives. When you are married, you find out day by day that your partner is not perfect. But if you can forgive your spouse, every day will be a new beginning, and every day will contain new joy. "Love bears all things, hopes and believes all things." Nothing is too heavy to carry if there is love. Even if a difficult situation confronts you as a couple, love will hold you firm with hope and faith, for it endures all things.

Faithfulness in marriage is of crucial importance for the inner life of each partner. There is a deep connection between married love in its spiritual and emotional aspects on the one hand, and sexual union on the other. When two people become one flesh in a true marriage, their physical uniting has a very deep connection with God. Should their sexual relationship become separated from him, it becomes a sinful thing even within marriage. Having a marriage certificate does not give one the freedom to live for the body and its appetites.

Because of the unique intimacy and mystery of the sexual sphere in marriage, an unparalleled uniting takes place when each partner surrenders completely to the other. This uniting is the organic expression of married love, whose very goal is the mutual giving of self. Each partner knows the secret of the other, and it is God's will that only this one man and this one woman keep that secret and do not pass it on to anyone else.

Our main calling is to follow Jesus, whatever the cost. If we are given the gift of a partner, it should double our dedication to Jesus, not weaken it. Marriage should lead us closer to Jesus.

We pray that those who enter marriage may allow nothing to separate them from the love of God, whatever may happen; for his love is always there to hold each of them and both of them together through need and suffering as well as through times of joy.

The bond of marriage is a promise to be faithful through thick and thin, through good days and hard days, and to be completely dependent on the love of God for the whole of life.

One of the greatest dangers in marriage is nagging – showing dissatisfaction over very little things because one feels one's partner is not perfect. If a person always thinks he is in the right, he will not be open to love. He might fear God and listen to his will and his Word, but the Enemy will always be watching to tempt him, even if in little things. When nagging begins in a marriage, love will slowly cool off. We must be aware of this danger. But if we are willing to dare all things, hope all things, and forgive all things, then every day will be a new experience of love, even if our marriage goes through hard days.

From a letter: I think you must seriously ask yourself
whether you have shown sufficient love and patience
to your wife, and whether you went out of your way
Eph. 5:23–29 to understand her situation and her needs. A husband
should lead the family, but this means that his first
duty is to understand the needs of his wife and

children. Without understanding them, he cannot show them love or give them leadership.

From a letter: When the situation between you and your husband becomes clear in your hearts before God, who alone sees everything, you will recognize that there are wrongs on both sides. Read 1 Corinthians 13:4–7 with your inner eye turned to your marriage:

1 Cor. 13:4–7

> Love is patient; love is kind and envies no one. Love is neither boastful nor conceited, neither rude nor selfish; not quick to take offense. Love keeps no score of wrongs, does not gloat over other's sins, but delights in the truth. There is nothing love cannot face; there is no limit to its faith, its hope, and its endurance.

If you read this, I think you will feel that both of you are guilty, and that you both have offended love in your marriage.

From a letter: I think you are right that your husband is wounded in his heart. You cannot heal his hurt, but you can humble yourself. Humility has a healing effect on a person whom we have hurt. The Bible says, "Wives, be subject to your husbands" and "The husband is the head of the family." (Eph. 5:22–24)

I know you have your own burden to carry, and you are right, you must lay it down at the foot of the cross so that healing and forgiveness can be given. Part of laying everything down at the cross is feeling sorry to the depths of our hearts for what we have done. I think of you both in great love and will pray for you.

From a letter: Dear brother, be absolutely silent before God, and listen with your heart to the voice of God. Seek him together with your wife. It is God who joined you together; it is God who will hold you together; it is God who will protect you.

Sex

The sexual aspect of marriage is by no means the most important part of the relationship. The significance of sex is exaggerated today in a thoroughly unhealthy way. Love between man and woman is seen too often only in an animal sense, as a sexual impulse, and its true significance is utterly missed.

Obviously, there are differences in the biological makeup of the male and the female. But it is completely materialistic to think that the difference between man and woman is merely biological. A woman longs to absorb her beloved one into herself. She is designed by nature to receive and to endure; to conceive, to bear, to nurse, and to protect. It is part of the evil of our time that women revolt against carrying the burden and pain of pregnancy and birth. A man, on the other hand, desires to enter into his beloved one and become one with her; he is made to initiate and penetrate rather than to receive.

A true man represents Christ as the head, even if he is a very weak person. But this must not be taken as if he were an overlord. His is the apostolic task: "Go out and gather! Teach people. Submerge them in the atmosphere of God, in the life of the Father, the Son, and the Holy Spirit." Women are in no way excluded from this task, but it is in a special way the duty of the man.

Mt. 28:19–20

It is quite clear that the differences between man and woman are not absolute. A true woman will represent Christ and the apostolic truth, and a true man will have in him the submission and humility of Mary.

Today's religion is psychology, and psychology analyzes man as an animal and not as an image of God. Freud is right on many points, but he forgets the main factor: God. Because he analyzes man as if he were not made in the image of God, he explains the sexual urge as man's motivating force. He even sees the relationship of child to father and mother as based on sex.

Psychologists are right in teaching that there are many urges in us – not only sexual urges, but also the desire for property and for power. But their conclusion that it is not good to suppress these urges is wrong. It completely ignores the reality of God and the fact that man was created in his image.

The love and unity between two people in a marriage is deeply symbolic. The Apostle Paul says, "I take it to mean Christ and the church." Such are the holy terms in which marriage is presented, and for this reason it needs to be completely subordinated to God. Its real nature can be understood only in relation to Christ and to eternity. The moment the sensual or sexual sphere is isolated from God and treated as an end in itself, the soul becomes defiled and sick. Certainly, sex is something distinct from love; yet there must be a deep harmony between sex and married love.

Eph. 5:32

Sex is intrinsically intimate and mysterious, and it should remain so because of its close connection with love, the deepest and most spiritual of all experiences. It would be a serious error to believe that when two people meant by God for each other become one flesh, it is solely for the purpose of procreation. It is simply not true that marriage is purposeful only in this limited sense.

In contrast to all other areas of bodily experience, the sphere of sex is deep in and of itself. Its sensuality has certain essential elements that penetrate to the very roots of man's physical being and directly into his soul. It has a depth and an earnestness that reaches far beyond the limits of the body and into the experiences of mind and spirit.

Therefore when a man surrenders himself to lust he is defiled in quite a different way than, for instance, by gluttony. Satisfying sexual lust wounds man in his innermost heart and being; it attacks and harms the soul at its core.

1 Cor. 6:13–17

The sexual aspect of the sensual sphere has a central place in man because there body, soul, and spirit meet as they do in no other area of human experience. Thus the sexual life has an intimacy all its own which the individual instinctively hides from others. Sex is *his* secret, something that he feels touches on his inmost being. Every disclosure in this sphere reveals something intimate and personal and lets another person into his secret. That is why the area of sex is also the area of shame: we are ashamed to unveil our secret before others.

How dreadful is a time and age in which man so despises himself and his human worth that all sense of shame is lost! To the pure man the sexual sphere is his own individual secret, and when it is uncovered, it is uniquely revealed as the complete surrender of self in wedlock to only one person.

The sex revolution of today is destroying the inner soul of man. We want to witness with our lives to something quite different: the fact that absolute purity and faithfulness in marriage are possible.

The whole idea of the sexual relationship between man and woman comes from God. It is nothing to be ashamed of; it is simply too holy to be constantly talked about.

Because of its unique nature, sex can take two very different forms: it can be an awe-inspiring, mysterious, noble, chaste, and peaceful act, in which case it will have a redeeming effect. But it can also be a forbidden surrender to naked lust, and then it will sicken the soul of man and become the domain of evil and of diabolical appeal.

Desecration of any sort is sin. If I abuse a human being by treating him as a thing instead of a human being, I violate his dignity as an image of God. It is desecration to seduce another human being with no thought of responsibility for his or her soul. It is a crime against the spirit, soul, and body of the other person *and* against oneself.

To seduce a person of the same sex is even more terrible. It is godless and perverse, and the Old and New Testaments, as well as the early church fathers, speak earnestly against it.

To enter marriage solely in order to satisfy physical desire is completely out of the question. But one cannot deny the senses entirely. When you hear lovely singing, you do not deny your sense of hearing. And when you see the beauty of God's creation, you do not deny your sense of sight. When you smell spring and flowers, you do not deny your sense of smell. The same is true of the sense of sex. Divorced from God, sex is horrible darkness; that is true. But if you try to deny it completely, you force yourself into something unnatural.

People come much too close to the fire of love and sex without any inner foundation. They go into sexual relationships lightly, without reverence for God, and their inner life is destroyed. Even faithfulness in marriage has become more and more uncommon. Yet God remains faithful, and he wants us to be faithful.

From a letter: Sex has no purpose apart from marriage. Outside of marriage it is sinful. The Bible demands chastity before it and outside of it; that is very clear. So if you have not always followed the chaste and pure way, then you must find forgiveness in order to stand upright before God. But Jesus wants to give you this forgiveness.

Celibacy

1 Cor. 7:32–35

We must recognize that to give up marriage is a great sacrifice. But to belong completely and undividedly to Christ is a great gift. In a sense, a relationship with Christ can acquire deeper meaning for a single person than for a married person, because his or her heart can be directed solely toward Christ, and a complete and undivided personal relationship with him is possible.

Christ compares the kingdom of God to a marriage banquet more than once. He calls the soul to union with him, and he wants to give himself undividedly to each person. There is nothing that surpasses the inner warmth, tenderness, and fruitfulness of unity with Jesus. This highest, most intimate bond of the soul can fill any void. Think, for instance, of the many believers through history who suffered in prison for years – even decades – for the sake of their faith. Through grace, each of us can find this bond of love and unity too.

Lk. 14:16–20

In Luke 14:16–20, Jesus speaks of those who reject his invitation to the banquet for love of other things. Ultimately, it is a matter of becoming totally undivided. In order to be wholly filled by God and completely free to follow him, we must be inwardly empty of all else. The danger of a divided heart is especially great when we are concerned with things or people worthy of love. When our inner eye is no longer directed toward Christ alone, then motherhood, fatherhood, family, children, and even the community of life and love in marriage can become idols that easily absorb our love.

We must give our hearts solely to God. Our love to him and to Christ must become so strong that we are joyfully prepared for any sacrifice. It is our prayer that we may die so that Christ may radiate from us; that we may no longer live for ourselves, but Christ in us.

From a letter: You ask if Jesus is calling you to renounce marriage for the sake of the kingdom of heaven. I believe that such a call to celibacy is possible, and not only for those with a Catholic background. But I would be hesitant to make such a vow hastily; it would have to be very carefully considered beforehand.

From a letter: I can well imagine your inner need and struggle in giving up marriage, though you should know that you are not the only one who has gone through pain and lacks inner peace in this question. Ultimately, we all have to be willing to be used by God as he wills. The thought that God does not love you is certainly of the devil. You are clinging too much to one great gift – marriage – while there are other much greater gifts that God also wants to give you. The greatest gift is a burning love to Christ. We should be willing to give up everything for this.

From a letter: In every human being there is the longing for a partner, and there is nothing wrong in this – it is put into man by God. Yet in discipleship to Jesus we can find the fulfillment of this longing without marriage, even if it is rarely given without great pain, many tears, and anguish of heart.

I wish for you that you might find such a healing in Christ – such a fullness and richness that there is no place in your life left void or empty. This is possible only through finding a deep dedication to Jesus himself and through feeling his grace in the depths of your heart.

May your life be guided only by Christ, in whatever way he wants it, so that when you come to the end of your life, or when Christ returns to this earth, you will stand as a prepared virgin with a trimmed lamp.

Family Life

Children

Mk. 10:14–15

Jesus said that only children – or those who are like them – will enter the kingdom of God. Unlike adults, children are not divided, dualistic beings. They are one whole; they are vulnerable; they are wholly dependent on father and mother. Christ calls us to become like children, and this means we must drop everything and become completely dependent on God and on one another.

cf. Mt. 18:3–6

If we as parents love God with all our heart and soul, our children will have the right reverence for us, and we will also have reverence for our children and for the wonderful mystery of becoming and being a child. Reverence for the spirit that moves between parent and child is the basic element of a true family life.

Mt. 18:1–3

The disciples came to Jesus and asked, 'Who is the greatest in the kingdom of heaven?' He called a child, set him in front of them, and said, 'I tell you this: unless you turn around and become like children, you will never enter the kingdom of heaven.'"

---

*For this chapter extensive use has been made of the author's pamphlet *The Purity of Childhood* (Plough, 1974).

These words of Jesus tell us what great value the soul of a little child has in the eyes of God. We can be sure
Lk. 12:7 that every hair of every child is counted by God, and
Mt. 18:10 that every child has a guardian angel who always has access to the throne of God.

The innocence of a child is an enormous blessing. However, there is an inclination to sin in every child, and therefore we must lead children in the right way so that they do not lose their childlikeness – that is,
Mt. 18:6 their purity of heart. It is a terrible crime to lead a child to sin.

It is very important for parents and educators to implant in each child a deep love for God, for Jesus, and for other people. Parents and educators should tell children about Jesus: how he was born in a stable, how he lived and worked, how he healed the sick, how he loved children and blessed them, how he died on the cross and rose again, and what significance the angel-world had in his life. It is important to have a childlike attitude toward the angel-world and toward the life of Jesus. Children experience spiritual things in a much more real and deep way than we suspect.

It is more important to lead children to a burning love for Christ than to teach them – much less force them – to say regular prayers that do not come from the heart each morning or evening. Children can learn to love God through songs and stories from the Bible and from hearing about the life of Jesus. The first task of parents and educators is to awaken in children a love for Christ. Then an inner urge to pray to him will also awaken in them.

It is no use to know the Bible inside out, or to make children learn it inside out, if God does not speak directly to the heart. We need to be very careful not to put religious pressure on children; we want them to have a simple, childlike attitude toward God, toward Jesus, and toward the Bible.

Just as we must cleanse our own hearts continually, so we must prepare the hearts of our children so that they may become good soil for the Word of God. God suffers when a heart is like a hard-trodden or rocky path, or when it is full of thorns. Preaching, however, does not make good soil; it often hardens the heart.

Our church has its own nurseries for our children from the age of six weeks and up, its own kindergartens and schools. But we do not believe that the church community has the main authority for educating children – the parents do. The home is the foundation of education. Those who care for children at school or elsewhere can only complement the spiritual atmosphere of the home.

A child's inner security begins in his relationship
Ex. 20:12 with his parents. The Ten Commandments do not say in vain, "Honor father and mother." We have found that when a child does not learn to honor his father and mother, he often finds it hard to fit into society in later life.

From a letter: For a child the fear of God must begin
Dt. 6:13 with fear of father and mother. The idea of fearing God is biblical, but this does not mean that a child should be afraid of his parents or afraid of God. It simply means he should have deep reverence, deep respect, and deep love for them.

From a letter: It has been said that the first four years of a child's life are the most crucial in his education.* If a child has reverence for his parents and for God when he is three or four years old, then the battle is won. But if his self-will is victorious at this age, it will be very difficult to overcome later.

*See Friedrich Wilhelm Foerster, *Hauptaufgaben der Erziehung* (Freiburg, 1959), p. 69.

From a letter: As regards children's education, I would say that in general I am wary of extremes – of the pendulum swinging from one side to the other, from hardness to softness, from depression to exaggerated joy, from a negative approach to a positive approach that no longer sees any real problems. One must find a way that tackles all difficulties in patience, joy, and loving clarity.

As parents we must overcome the illusion that our children are good. We must be careful not to have too rosy a view of them, and we must not be touchy if someone questions their behavior. We must love our children so much that we are ready to fight for their souls.

From a letter: You say that you feel completely helpless in connection with your child's difficult behavior. Please do not hide behind this excuse. All of us are helpless and dependent on God; you are no different. But it is a sin to throw up your hands and cry out, "We are helpless." As parents, you are called by God to help your child and to love him, but also to fight for him and to be firm or even strict when necessary. The main thing is for you to win your child's heart.

From a letter: You are concerned about your children's selfishness, self-centeredness, and unpeacefulness. Take a firm stand against these things. Because your children want to be the center of attention, they become, as you write, bossy, touchy, and disrespectful. Turn away from the softness that you have confessed; but don't become harsh. That is not the answer either. You must find the right firmness in God's love. He does not tolerate the things you speak of. We fail our children when our emotional feelings and ties push us around.

From a letter: I plead with you to fight for your children. There is no reason for despair if one fails again and again. One must simply keep up the fight. It cannot be tolerated that a child goes to the dogs. Be compassionate, be strict, be gentle again. It will not always be easy going, but you are responsible before God for your children.

From a letter: I want to encourage you to have patience with your children. A certain sharpness toward children is healthy, but impatience is not. May God give us patient hearts.

From a letter: Thank you for your letter about your son. His behavior is quite normal for a two-year-old. In my own upbringing, if my parents said something, then they meant it, and there was no way around it. This does not mean that we were always obedient at two years of age. But later it would have been unthinkable for us to disobey our father or mother. They were not hard on us, but they were firm, and they did not tolerate the slightest doubt that they meant what they said.

From a letter: Thank you for your letter in which you tell about the trouble you have with your three-year-old son. Children at this young age need an inwardly sure hand. Outbursts of sharpness are not good for them, but serious, firm, and kind leadership will help.

From a letter: It is quite natural that the difficult situation with your daughter pains you. It would be unnatural if a mother did not feel such pain. But use it to deepen your faith in God, in Christ, and in the church. Then you will be able to find faith for your daughter and help her.

Augustine, the mystic, lived a sinful life as a young man, but he had a very devout mother, Monica, who did not stop believing and praying for him until he broke down and repented. Later he became a servant of Christ, and for centuries he has influenced people in their search for God. I wish you the faith of Monica. It begins with the pain you are now suffering. In spite of all our pain, God is always greater. I greet you with much love.

From a letter: It is not a good trend that in our century such important mysteries of life as the birth of a baby are explained in a purely scientific way. Even if we can give a biological explanation, and even if we can explain how two cells grow in the mother's womb, this is only half the truth. The most important things – the coming of a soul, the first smile, the capacities of the human heart and the riches it can experience – can never be explained. We stand before the invisible reality of eternity.

It can be damaging to a child to tell him too much about sex, birth, and death, and everything must be done to avoid it. We definitely do not mean that children should be brought up as prudes. But we believe that birth and death exist only in connection with the world of heaven and that they should be explained to children only in relation to God.

In spite of all that is wonderful about children, we must recognize that because they are human, they have inherited an inclination to sin. Whether it takes the form of lying, stealing, a lack of reverence for parents and educators, or sexual impurity, evil must be fought in every child.

We must be careful not to spoil our children, even from a very early age. It harms a child's character to bring him up indulgently. Flabbiness is a sign of selfishness, and selfishness always leads to sin. Softness can also arise through an unhealthy emotional relationship between a child and his parent or educator.

How to fight against sin in children is a very difficult question. If there are indecencies, for example, which mostly begin with children exposing themselves to each other and sometimes touching each other, the child will feel instinctively that this is not right. These indecencies almost always involve lying. We must be careful not to make too much of such things among children. It may only draw their attention to the sexual area all the more. The best thing, perhaps, is to give them a small punishment and so close the matter, and then help them to think of other things.

We grown-ups too easily forget that many things do not mean the same to a child as they do to us, and we must never project our ideas and feelings and experiences onto a child's mind. We must also never forget that it is in a certain way natural for children to go through periods of sexual curiosity. This cannot be mistaken for sin. But we should lead our children in such a way that their souls remain pure and innocent. Too much questioning can harm a child, because through fear he may become more and more entangled in lies.

It is a great injustice to label children or adolescents, especially those who have offended in the sexual area. In our assessment of childish offenses, we should beware of coming too quickly to harsh conclusions about the character of a child and his future development. Rather, we should help him to find new interests and to make a joyful new beginning.

We know that we can find the way to the heart of any child by appealing to his conscience. Every child has an instinctive longing in his heart for a pure conscience, and we should support this longing, for he will suffer if his conscience is burdened.

There is a certain point at which a child is no longer a child in the true sense of the word. The moment he sins consciously, he ceases to be a child. It is then the task of his parents and teachers to help him find repentance, the experience of Jesus on the cross, and a conversion that leads to the forgiveness of sins. Through the cross a lost childhood *can* be restored.

From a letter: There is no question that children differ in how they learn. Some children learn more through hearing, some through feeling, some through seeing, and so on. We must try to be just toward each child. We do not want to push every child toward an academic career; that would be out of the question. The main thing is that a child is surrounded by love.

Academic work should and must be done, but woe to us if it is done at the expense of the childlike heart, or of the child himself. The stupid arrogance of teachers who think of themselves and others of their choosing as intellectually gifted, to the exclusion of still others, is pure sin. We must be ruled by Christ, the head of the Body. In him is true childlikeness, compassion, and mercy.

From a letter to a young child: In order to hear Jesus speak to us, it is important to listen to our hearts. When we feel love to God and to Jesus, to our father and mother and brothers and sisters, that is the voice of Jesus.

Youth

It is a privilege to lead young people to Jesus, to show them how marvelous God's world is despite the terrible impurity, corruption, and darkness of our age. For young people it is especially important that their reverence for God and their respect for father and mother is never extinguished, even if they do sin consciously.

Parents must seek a relationship of trust with their children from earliest childhood on and not wait until problems arise, say around the age of five or six. If they wait too long, they may be able to gain outward obedience only and not the inner response and respect necessary to solve problems like lying, indecency, and disobedience. But if a relationship of trust and respect is achieved, it will be impossible for a child to resist his parents.

Some young people go through more difficult periods of development than others, and we must be careful not to be too harsh and judgmental toward them. The main thing is that they are led to repentance, conversion, and faith. I do not believe that this can be achieved through hard punishment. As long as there is even a little flame of reverence for God and parents within them, the way to their hearts will remain open. However, where the last spark of reverence has been extinguished in a young person, one can only fight for conversion through prayer. We must remember that conversion can never be brought about by persuasion.

From a letter: Your son is now an adolescent, and you have a big responsibility. I would tell him that the magnetic powers of attraction between boys and girls are quite natural, but that they must be ruled by God and reserved for the one person whom God might later give him in marriage. You can also tell him about the physical relationship between husband and wife. I think you have already laid a good foundation for his knowledge of the facts of life, but in high school he will hear plenty about these things, and it is better he hears them from you first.

From a letter: I would speak very clearly and openly to your son about the physical changes he will go through, and tell him that if he keeps his body pure now, it will not be difficult later in life. If he is not able to keep himself pure now, he will have a hard struggle later. I would also tell him that sex is meant only for marriage. There is no other place for it, and he should keep himself pure for the one girl God may one day give him. It may not be easy to put this into words – everything you say must be said in the light of God and with reverence for him. But I am sure he will show you the right way.

My father always had an open heart for young people, but he never made concessions to worldliness or eroticism. Having a big heart never means making concessions to the devil.

From a letter to a 17-year-old: Dear brother, I am glad that you want to make a new beginning. I think you have been a very proud young man. Read the Old and

New Testaments, and you will see how pride hinders God from speaking to man and working in him. Your everyday life has revolved around yourself, though I thank God that you now want to turn away from your self-centeredness. Be an example of dedication and humility, and be a witness for Jesus at the high school. This is something so badly needed in our time.

From a letter: I often think of the words of Jesus,
Mt. 16:26 "What good is it for a man to gain the whole world at the price of his soul?" especially when I see what our youth is taught today in the area of psychology. I am afraid for their souls. What makes me uneasy is that man's lower instincts are put in the center and viewed as harmless simply because they are natural. It is a terrible thing to teach people about the human soul without teaching them about its relationship to God.

From a letter to a disabled child: You have a weak body, but you have a living soul. Thank God for this. There are many people in this world who have a strong body and a dull soul. Actually all people, even if they are strong and healthy, depend on God and on Jesus. Only sometimes they do not realize it. The wonderful thing is that you do. Hold firmly to this, and Jesus will lead you through everything.

From a letter: You are never too young to give your life to Jesus, and you are never too young to feel his closeness. I am thankful that you want to give everything up to God and that you want to be humble. Hold on to this longing through all struggles–your life will surely bring them, for there is no life of discipleship without need and struggle. I wish you the protection of God in all you may go through. May the pierced hands of Jesus hold you firmly as you hold firmly to him.

From a letter: You are right; the main thing is not joining our church, but following Christ. If you are clear about this, God will show you the way to do it best. We will support you even if your way is not the way of community.

From a letter: To think only about God's unending patience and forgiveness makes him into something quite different from what he really is. God is to be feared: it is terrible to fall into his hands. Your idea of God is not God; it is the tool of an impudent young woman. You have been running your own life. I plead with you to have reverence for the wrath of God.

From a letter: It is good to realize that following Jesus may cost much suffering and perhaps even death for his sake. In this connection you must take a stand against the evil you meet in the world, also at the high school. I can well understand that there is a lot that tempts you, especially in the way of impurity. But if you take a stand for Jesus, his clear light will give you a disgust for all sin. May Jesus guide you every day, and may you never stray from his will.

From a letter to a 13-year-old: Already at your age you have to make a decision either for or against Jesus. If you do not decide for him, you will decide against him. This is simply a fact; you cannot sit on the fence.

From a letter to a college student: Jesus says that he is
Jn. 10:14–15 the good shepherd and that his sheep know him and know his voice. You belong to his flock, and I hope you find moments of quiet to hear his voice for inner refreshment. I know there are many things in the city that distract you and tire you out, including the many hours you have to work every day. But it remains that your inner life is more important than your getting a degree, even if you are already very close to reaching that goal. I encourage you to hold on. It is good for one's character to stick something out to the end.

Family Ties

Christ laid down his life for the church, and he loves her deeply. But he is also the Savior of the church, and
Eph. 5:22–33 the church is subject to him. In marriage, the bride is compared to the church and the bridegroom to Christ. Christ loves his church not only with gentle words: he
Rv. 2:16, 23 also disciplines her with sharpness. We must be careful that a soft emotionalism does not enter our family life, either between husband and wife or between parents and children. Emotionalism ruins the Christlike clarity in a relationship.

From a letter: I understand your struggle to fulfill the commandment to honor father and mother. You write that you love your father very much, and that is the main thing–that is the same as honoring him. But the fact that you have to disapprove of his ways is also
Lk. 14:26 right and true before God. Jesus says, "If anyone comes to me and does not hate his own father and mother, wife and children, brothers and sisters–yes, his own life–he cannot be my disciple." The word "hate" should not shock you. Jesus does not teach hatred. Here "hate" means taking a stand against something wrong. If you accept both this passage and the
Ex. 20:12 command "Honor father and mother" as a guide, I think you will find the right attitude to your father and mother.

Jesus' demand for holiness reaches even into the closest
family relationships. He says, "Anyone who loves his
Mt. 10:37–38 father or mother more than me is not worthy of me;
anyone who loves his son or daughter more than me is
not worthy of me; and anyone who does not take his
cross and follow me is not worthy of me." If we want
to be disciples of Jesus we must take these words seri-
Mt. 10:39 ously. Jesus also says, "By gaining his life, a man will
lose it, but by losing his life for my sake, he will gain
it." So if we lose ourselves completely for Jesus' sake,
we will gain eternal life. But if we cling to our own
ideas and ideals, to our property, family, or children,
we will lose everything.

From a letter: I think you have tied your grown children too tightly to yourself, which has also brought division between you and your husband. Your daughters were not free before God. Parents must give their children freedom already when they are small, but even more so when they have grown up. I do not mean freedom to do evil, but freedom from all emotional ties that bind them in a wrong way to father and mother.

We need to learn the meaning of Jesus' words, "He
Lk. 14:26 who does not hate father, mother, wife, and children
cannot be my disciple." Jesus does not mean a feeling
1 Jn. 3:15 of hatred; the New Testament says, "He who hates his
brother is a murderer." Jesus means that we must put

him first, above the emotional ties of family life. Often these emotional ties are mixed with mammonism, though not always. We must be sharp on ourselves and take the decisive stand of Christ. It is clear that a family without love is godless, but a family ruled by the clouded emotions of blood-ties will have no love to God and Christ. Let us love one another only with the love of Christ and the love of the Holy Spirit. Then the God-given ties between father, mother, and children will have his blessing.

Illness and Death

From a letter: All sickness is a form of evil, yet we must accept it as from God's hand. It is a paradox–a paradox that we can also see on the cross. The cross was God's way of redeeming man, but it was also a work of the devil.

From a letter: I can well understand the fear you feel in the face of your upcoming operation; I would also be afraid. But I believe that you are in the hands of God

Jn. 14:1–4

and that he understands your fear. In the Bible there are endless encouraging verses which tell us not to fear but to remain firm in God. That is what I wish for you. Give your life trustingly into his hands.

From a letter: I would advise you not to be so worried about your health. It would drive the healthiest person crazy to constantly feel his pulse or listen to his heartbeat. The real question is your fear of death and the unknown. Most probably you will still live a number of decades. But you will have to face the question of eternity. All of us should live life so as to be able to face eternity at any time. Shortly before my aunt died, she seemed to glimpse eternity, and she said, "It is so wonderful–so wonderful! It is so much more real than life down here on earth." This attitude was the fulfillment of a dedicated life. I wish you this and greet you with love.

From a letter: You write that you seem to be going downhill physically. But I believe that Jesus will help you with his love and power, if not through physical healing, then by giving you inner peace and joy to bear your sickness. I thank God that you are always able to find inner peace in turning to Jesus. It is a gift that you can see your need as small, at least in the face of the need of the whole world. Such a recognition can come only from God. I pray for strength and guidance for you.

From a letter: Don't fall prey to your dark and fearful thoughts. If you are afraid of everything–afraid of yourself, your weakness, your sinfulness, afraid of other people, afraid of making mistakes, and on and on–your soul will become sick.

You are right in saying, "The only true healing is faith in Jesus." What a wonderful truth this is! In Jesus all fears vanish. Hold on to this.

Jas. 5:14–16 James writes that if someone is seriously ill, he should call the elders of the church, and they should pray for him and anoint him with oil in the name of the Lord.

He also writes in this connection, "Confess your sins to one another and pray for one another, and you will find healing; for the true prayer of the righteous has real power."

In this sense we intercede for someone who is very ill with the laying on of hands, anointing him in order to give him our full inner support and full forgiveness – if there is anything to be forgiven. No matter how serious his illness, his life is in the arms of God and the church.

From a letter: What must we do to receive the gift
1 Cor. 12:9 of healing? In 1 Corinthians 12 it clearly says that the gift of healing is given to the church, although not to every member. The condition for receiving such a great gift is spiritual poverty and a pure heart before God. So if the gift of healing is not given to us, it is very possibly our own fault. But it also might be that it is not God's will.

The powerful gift of healing which God gave the Blumhardts* was remarkable. Yet at the end of his life the younger Blumhardt withdrew more and more from using this gift, because he felt God was no

---

*Johann Christoph Blumhardt (1805–1880), south-German pastor, author, and theologian; Christoph Friedrich Blumhardt (1842–1919), his son and successor.

longer being honored in the miraculous healings that took place. People were healed, but only in the flesh. And afterward they talked and boasted about their healing. Some were even honored and glorified for it. Blumhardt felt that unless healing was accompanied by repentance, God could no longer work through him.

Blumhardt's attitude should challenge us: when God gives us a gift, he wants us to accept it quietly. If the grace of healing is given to us, we ourselves should not be honored; God should be honored.

Blumhardt often warned, "When grace is given to you, keep it a secret between you and God, and don't make a religious show of it. Remain natural and honor God." He also emphasized that healing is not the most important thing; sickness is no sin. It is more important to give your life to God, even if you are sick, than to be healed and then forget God. "If God heals you, be joyful, but be just as joyful in sickness."

From a letter: In these last days God has spoken to us all through the sudden death in your family. We want to carry your pain with you. I know it will not go away quickly. But it may be God's will that it doesn't. Pain deepens something in one's heart and life.

After the death of a baby: It is very hard to understand why a human life is sent by God to live on earth for only one hour. We stand here before a mystery that

God alone understands. We may ask, "Why did this happen? Why? Why?" Only God knows. And we believe in him and in his Son, the good shepherd, also for little lambs such as this tiny baby.

Shortly before the death of the author's child: We simply do not know what the will of God is – whether this child is destined for life or not – but we do know that if it is his will, the child will become healthy. I feel it as a promise, after the doctors have said they can do nothing, that if we believe, Jesus Christ can do anything. In some way, through this little child, the will of God and the mercy of God will be shown. Only when man ceases to be able to do anything can the work of Christ begin. He can work only when we give him our trust and our faith completely and without reserve. We should depend on nothing material or external, neither on money nor on doctors, but on Jesus Christ alone.

After the death of the author's child: Death is destruction; death is division and separation. But Jesus unites, and perfect life means perfect unity. Where Jesus is at work, unity is created. Therefore we challenge all to take part in this unity. Those who do not gather, scatter and separate, and those who separate and destroy serve death. But those who unite serve Jesus, and one day he will gather them into eternity.

From a letter: Dear sister, I can well understand that you still suffer under the loss of your father. It is never easy to cope with death and the need it brings; death is the enemy of God and will be overcome only at the last resurrection.

But we must also see that for those who have followed Christ, death means closeness to him. It is understandable that the thought of eternity shakes you. But you should not look fearfully into the future. Give everything over to Jesus.

From a letter: I am very sorry that you have to bear such a heavy loss. A painful experience like this, the death of your child, always reminds us that this earth is not yet fully our home, nor will be until Jesus Christ is its only ruler, and sin, death, sorrow, fear, and pain are completely overcome and vanquished. But until that day – the greatest of all days – we can be sure that your child and all children are in Jesus' hands.

In regard to the question of praying for someone who has died, I have to admit that I do not know just what the right answer is. I don't know whether you are familiar with the following passage from the Gospel of John, or whether you have ever accepted it in your heart. It says:

Jn. 5:24–28

> Truly, I say to you, he who hears my word and believes Him who sent me, has eternal life; he does not come into judgment but has passed from death to life. Truly, I say to you, the hour is coming, and now is, when the dead will hear the voice of the Son of God, and those who hear will live. For as the Father has life in himself, so he has granted the Son also to have life in himself and has given him authority to execute judgment, because he is the Son of Man. Do not marvel at this; for the hour is coming when all who are in the tombs will hear his voice.

Read this passage and consider it deeply before God. Perhaps it will show you the depth of his love.

All men fear death. But Christ promises something that overcomes death and stands through all eternity: his eternal love. Here is something that reaches into the depths of being and into future paths of forgiveness–despite even physical death–and leads us into the kingdom of God.

It is our daily prayer to experience Jesus as dwelling within us. But we know that he also sits at the right hand of the Father and rules over angel-worlds, powers, and principalities, as well as over his church.

We can only have an inkling of the supercosmic greatness of these mysterious realities.

Jesus told his disciples in farewell that he would prepare a place for them. (Jn. 14:2) It remains an awe-inspiring mystery what this place is, and what is happening there in eternity, in the star-worlds and angel-worlds, and among the souls who have died in Christ. When Stephen was being stoned, he saw the heavens open and Jesus standing at the right hand of God, (Acts 7:55) and later John saw Jesus with flaming eyes. (Rv. 1:14) I believe that when Jesus comes again, we, too, will see him in person.

The basic relationship of man to God, of which all other relationships are merely likenesses, is stronger than any human relationship. Ultimately, we stand before God. This shows most plainly when a person faces death. Anyone who has been at the bedside of a dying person knows how absolute in its significance is man's inner relationship and original bond with God; he realizes that in the end, when his last breaths are drawn, this relationship is the *only* thing that counts.

We know from the Gospels that love to God cannot be separated from love to one's neighbor. Man's way to God is through his brother. I have experienced it myself at deathbeds that if a man lives completely for his fellowmen, then God will be very close in the last hour, too.

From a letter: The fact that your son has had to bear so much suffering and pain already as a child will certainly be of great importance for his whole life, and also for yours. That children have to suffer is very strange. It is as if they are bearing someone else's guilt, as if they are suffering because of the fall of creation. In a way they seem to be paying the wages of sin–sin in which they have taken no part. I have often thought this over, and I believe that perhaps the suffering of children has a close connection with the greatest suffering ever endured: God's suffering, Christ's suffering for lost creation. For they are closest to the heart of Jesus, and he points to them as an example for us. That is why I believe that the suffering of an innocent child always has great significance for the church.

In times of suffering, the most important thing is to keep and protect your inner joy, which is Jesus, the risen one. Then his power, which is the power of light, will also be the power of healing.

The fight of any individual against sickness or death shows us the struggle in which we all are placed–the struggle against darkness. When an attack of darkness comes upon us, we must put ourselves completely on the side of the light of Jesus. We should not despair when human strength ceases, for it is just at that moment that Christ can begin. As we read in the Gospel
Jn. 12:35 of John, "The light is with you yet a little while. Walk while you have the light, lest darkness come upon you."

Evil and Darkness

We are living in a time when many people either belittle evil or don't believe it exists at all. Because of this they understand neither the greatness of Golgotha nor the heaviness of God's final judgment. This judgment, which is described in the Revelation of John, cannot be understood unless we grasp the power of evil. If evil is seen as nothing especially serious, then there is no need to put up a serious fight against it.

The cross would not have been necessary if the power of evil were not so terrible. I have heard people ask, "Why couldn't God forgive sin without the sacrifice of Jesus?" This is a tempting question, but once we recognize the immense power of the evil that God had to fight, we will know there is no forgiveness without the cross.

There are people who try to understand the depths and secrets of Satan or who try to discover the source of evil. Certainly this is understandable, but it is not godly. The hearts of too many people in our society are burdened and troubled with what they have learned about murder, fornication, and other evils. A true Christian should be a child toward evil and have no experience in its secrets.

Modern man thinks too materialistically; he does not see that there is a power of good and a power of evil quite apart from him, and that the course of his life depends on the power to which he opens his heart.

As a young man I lived in Nazi Germany, and I knew people there who were actually quite harmless but who were gripped and driven by something very evil. And even though there were many–more than we know–who died in protesting this evil, the majority gave in to it. It was not only a few men ruling over a nation; Germany was ruled by evil spiritual powers or demons.

We believe that today, as in Christ's time, demons can be driven out and away and that when Christ returns to the earth, all men will live in complete freedom, although judgment must certainly take place first.

We run into the occult again and again, especially in colleges and high schools. Yet we sharply reject any form of contact with demonic powers, and we warn our children against such contact too. There are things of Satan which we should know nothing about. To put it plainly, we should be ignorant of those things. We simply do not want to know anything about them. Nowadays occultism is often regarded as just another science to be studied. But we want nothing to do with it.

A person who lives a childlike life in Jesus does not need to fear possession by an evil spirit. On the other hand, someone who has practiced magic or sorcery
Rv. 22:15 does have reason to be afraid. We reject even the most "harmless" forms of spiritualism, as well as superstitious practices such as wearing health rings, tipping tables, or talking with the dead. These things may start innocently, but they can bind a person to Satan without his realizing it. They have nothing to do with a childlike faith in Jesus.

We ask for God's judgment so that his light may break in. The more strongly his light breaks in and the more strongly the love of his only begotten Son burns in our hearts, the more clearly will his truth be revealed. When Jesus comes and touches men with his light, it means judgment as well as freedom and redemption. All doubts, all things that chain and burden men, all the sins that hold them down, are touched, and men are freed. This freeing and redemption brought about by the breaking in of Christ's light is given to the whole world, as is also the faith brought by him. For
Jn. 12:47 Christ said that he came not to judge the world but to save it.

Christ wants those who are most oppressed and desolate to turn to the light and be saved. Just those who are most crushed, who feel themselves most unworthy and burdened, should allow themselves to be touched and moved by God's great love. And once

they feel it, they will know that they are included and freed by it. They are the very ones Jesus took to himself: the evil-doers, the tax collectors, the prosti-
Mt. 8:16–17 tutes, the despised of men. He did not criticize those
Mt. 9:9–12 who were possessed; he freed them. But in their freeing was judgment, for darkness was revealed and driven out. Evil was in no way ignored, but men were freed from it.

From a letter: Until Jesus comes back and frees us completely, we will always have to fight sin on this earth. This fight is first a struggle against the lower nature. Second, it is a battle of spirits, a battle against Satan and his demons. Your fall was not only a matter of your lower nature; it was also satanic. The Bible says
Lk. 22:3 that when Judas betrayed Jesus, "Satan entered into him." I would not dare to say this about you, but I do think your situation tends in that direction. I do not think Satan could have entered Judas if Judas had not sold himself to him first. Judas had already gone to the high priest; he had already accepted the silver pieces when he went to the paschal meal with Jesus, where Satan entered into him.

Even if this comparison is too strong to apply to you, you did open your heart to evil powers. Where and when did this begin? Do not forget that true remorse is a wonderful experience, not one to be feared. If you experience real repentance, you will be grateful for it your whole life long.

It is a horrifying thing that man, who was created in the image of God, has built bombs that have the power to wipe out millions of people in a very short time. We must repent! The fact that our country has such weapons shows the need for us to dedicate ourselves to something completely different. For some people it might mean politics – working and fighting for the election of responsible citizens who would never use these weapons. We have great respect for this. But our opposition must be much deeper. The spirit that drives men to build weapons is evil, and we can fight it only by living for the good spirit.

We cannot go the way of Jesus without personal change. If we claim to follow him but live in impurity, for example, then we have no right to speak out against
Eph. 6:10 ff. things such as injustice. We are not fighting against flesh and blood – good people against evil people – but against powers and principalities of darkness.

If we commit a sinful act, we give room to an evil demon in our own life and surroundings. We have to
Lk. 8:30 see this realistically: evil is not something abstract. In the Bible, some demons even have names. There is no excuse for anyone, especially for someone who claims to be a committed Christian, to give room to demons or to serve them in any way. If he does, they will harm not only him but the community around him.

Eph. 5:25 *From a letter:* The life of the church is something extremely precious and important to Jesus. Thus the danger of Satan attacking the soul of the church is constant and very great. Blumhardt* writes that when Jesus was commissioned by the heavenly Father to bring forth children of light, he foresaw that Satan would follow him and produce children of evil, and that these children of evil would flourish even inside the church of Christ in the soil where only children of light should grow. This is very terrible, but it is something we have to face. It is most likely to happen when human power takes over where Christ's power alone should rule.

Jesus said that all men will "see the Son of Man seated
Mk. 14:62 at the right hand of the Power." He calls his Father "the Power." That is the greatest reality – a much greater reality than our mortal life. If we are afraid of the Evil One (and such fear can be very real) we can always trust in Jesus. He too is real. He is at the heart of the
Col. 1:15–20 throne of God. He *is* the heart of the church, the head of the church, and he understands our hearts, which we ourselves do not understand.

It is a great mistake to think that we can understand our own hearts. We may understand ourselves superficially, but only God really knows our hearts. Therefore, even if we suffer the severest temptations, trials, and

*See footnote p. 190.

attacks by the Evil One, we can always turn to God with trust and great hopes for victory.

Peace can be found only in the crucified one. Not even the united church is enough. The only place we can find peace and rest is Golgotha. We ourselves cannot wash away a murderous or an adulterous act. The only way to become free from darkness is to turn to the light, confess our sin, and come to the cross.
Rv. 7:14 There, as we read in Revelation, the blood of Christ can cleanse us.

From a letter: I have heard your desperate cry for help, and I have great understanding for you. Your thoughts frighten you so much that they gain power over you. You must turn from this fear. Through it you yourself suggest these thoughts into your heart, and then even more desperate and terrible fears, anxieties, and needs enter you.

Don't let your fears shake you. If you can drop them and trust in God, many things will become different. Never doubt in God's help and intervention. I assure you that he loves you and that he is much closer to you than you know.

Mt. 28:20 Jesus promises us that he will be with us always, until the end of all days. But we should not underestimate the dark powers of impurity, mammonism, murder, hatred, and unforgiveness surrounding us, which attack brothers and sisters in the church. Jesus must

Mt. 16:18

have foreseen that the church would be attacked by the powers of hell, because he told Peter that these powers would not overcome it. We need to watch and pray all the time.

Together with the rest of suffering humankind, we long that the demonic net that still covers the earth be rent–even if it means great turmoil. We believe it *will* be removed in God's time through the breaking in of his kingdom.

The Fight

The invisible powers that surround us men on earth can bring either great suffering or great joy. There are powers of God that bring peace, justice, joy, forgiveness of sins, and community. These powers are embodied in Jesus Christ. But there are also dark powers of murder, envy, ambition, and injustice. They, too, are invisible, but once they take hold of a person's soul, they drive him to commit visible deeds of evil.

We must grasp that the powers we are talking about are not abstract just because they are invisible. We are dealing with something absolutely real – not with a philosophy or a teaching, but with powers of darkness and light, good and evil, destruction and unity; with powers that want to kill and powers that want to make us alive.

When Jesus drove out devils from people who were possessed, he healed their souls and hearts. His
Lk. 11:15 enemies said, "He drives out the devil with a greater devil." But Jesus answered, "If I were to drive out
Lk. 11:17–18 the devil with a greater devil, his kingdom would be divided and would collapse." The devil's army is very disciplined: it knows how to attack a soul, a united group of people, or even a nation.

We know from the Gospel that the whole earth is a battlefield for God and the devil, and so is every human heart. We simply have to reckon with it that the devil will be furious when two or three or more are completely united in Jesus.

There was never a fiercer battle between God and Satan than that fought by Jesus at Golgotha. It even seemed to Jesus that God had forsaken him. But in spite of this, he laid his soul and spirit into the hands of the Father in trust. Then the victory was won, not only for this earth but for all powers, principalities, and angels.

From a letter: Our fight is not against flesh and blood, not against people; it is a fight for the atmosphere of the true church – for the atmosphere of God in each of our communities and in the heart of each brother and sister. All of us go through pain and judgment, but this should not be the end; judgment is only the beginning of new joy, hope, and the victory of redemption. It should free us for love, for service, and for God.

The atmosphere in any church must continually be renewed to become an atmosphere of love, purity, and everything else Jesus represented. Only then can love stream out from us to all people. For this we must pray and fight again and again.

The idea that Jesus brought a new philosophy or founded a religion is completely false. His person, his spirit, his cause, his healing, is not a philosophy

like that of the Greeks or Egyptians. He was and is a person, and it is he himself who meets us. I love the
Jn. 6:53 words, "Unless you eat the flesh of the Son of Man and drink his blood, you have no life in you." That is not the philosophy of some great man; it is Jesus himself.

No one can be indifferent to Jesus. One must decide for him or against him. The fact that we are sinful does not hinder us from coming to Jesus. Being tempted will not hinder us from coming to him either. Even if the Evil One torments us, that will not hinder us. But we cannot tolerate indifference to Jesus, and neither can we tolerate any human effort to interpret him. If we experience – not in our minds but in our
Jn. 1:29 hearts – the meaning of the words "This is the Lamb of God, who carries the sins of the world" or "For the
Heb. 9:15 forgiveness of sins he took this death upon himself," we will see that it is not a philosophy, but life.

We need to experience Jesus in his height and depth and breadth. And we must understand the cross, which stood firm and still stands, in a spiritual sense. It reaches up into heaven, to the throne of God, and its outstretched arms are still there for a lost humankind.

From a letter: Brothers and sisters, let us be wide awake, because whenever God wants to do something good among men, the devil makes every effort to destroy it. Think of the temptation of Jesus after his baptism: he was tempted by the devil because his heart was so pure, and because he belonged completely to God.

Nothing is more annoying to the prince of this world than a church in its first love. In Revelation, we
Rv. 2–3 can read how already in John's time the devil succeeded in harming the church. This happened to such an extent that Jesus had to tell one congregation that it
Rv. 3:1 only had the name of being alive, but was in fact dead. Yet even then he gave that church a chance to wake up, to change, and to return to a true and genuine love.

I believe – if I dare speak from my deepest heart – that Jesus wants to come to us as intimately as if his blood were our blood, to cleanse us completely.

From a letter: I protest against the idea that it is wrong to react with strong emotion or excitement when God is attacked, when brothers and sisters are mistreated, or
Jn. 2:12–17 when the church is harmed. I do not think Jesus was calm and collected when he drove the money changers out of the temple, where God's honor was at stake. I will protest my whole life long against cool soberness in the face of cruelty or anything else that destroys God's work.

In our concern for God's work, the tendency to judge men in a theoretical way is one of the gravest temptations. We need such an outpouring of the spirit of

God upon us that everything in us and among us is revealed. Following this, clarity and decisiveness will come of themselves. We must beseech God most earnestly for this love to Christ so that all darkness and evil in our household is revealed.

If we give ourselves over in faith to God and to Jesus, we will be cleansed. In his farewell words, Jesus
Jn. 15:5 says, "I am the true vine; you are the branches." He
Jn. 15:1–2 says that if we are to bear fruit, we will need to be cleansed, and the knife of the gardener will need to cut into our hearts. As disciples of Jesus we need this cleansing, this knife, this sharpness in our hearts and our lives. If we reject the gardener who cleanses us, we are unfaithful in the eyes of God, and we will not be able to bear fruit.

Are we ready to have Christ's Word cut deeply into us, or will we repeatedly protect and harden ourselves against it? We do not realize how often we stand in God's way. But we can ask him in his mercy and love to cut us with his Word – even if it hurts.

We should put our whole trust in God alone. Yet we also need to trust one another. We cannot live without trusting one another, even though we know that men
Jn. 18:15–27 can and do fail. Peter denied Jesus three times, yet he

was one of the most trusted apostles. He failed, but then he went away and wept bitterly. There is no other way for us either, than to repent as deeply and to weep as bitterly as he did.

Even if we have to recognize that we have failed, we must not see everything as black – or think the foundation has been taken away from under our lives. God's judgment is God's goodness; it cannot be separated from his mercy and compassion. If we repent deeply and become humble before God, we will become nothing, and then Christ can live in us.

It is certainly sinful to use God's working in us to build up our own pride. But it is also sinful to deny God's working when we fail him. Our failures should lead us to humility and to God.

Perhaps the worst thing that can be said against a church is what was written to the church at Sardis:
Rv. 3:1 "Though you have the name of being alive, you are dead." If a church is dead, it is like the salt spoken of in the Sermon on the Mount, which has lost its taste and will be thrown away and trodden upon. Every church is in danger of going to sleep, of losing its life. Yet Jesus says that if he finds life even in a few, he will have patience and give them time to repent.

In the short history of our community we have known the struggle for purity in our church. We have known the struggle against deadness and against being a church that has the name of being alive but is in actual fact dead. Yet each time Jesus chastises us, he gives us time to repent, as a church and as individuals.

Mt. 5:13

One passage in the Gospel has become very clear to us: we must be salt. We have realized with a shudder how dangerous it is for the church if the flavor and power of its salt is lost. Salt gives taste to something tasteless, and salt wards off decay. Our age needs salt.

We are guilty of having tolerated false spirits for too long. Jesus warns us very sharply against false prophets and against those who speak of peace where there is no peace, or of love where there is no love.

From a letter: We must find the way to follow Jesus' command to forgive others just as he forgives us, but at the same time we must be clear and let no darkness come into the church. This is sometimes a great tension for me. In Colossians 3:12–17, Paul says that we should have understanding, forgiveness, and kindness in our hearts toward our brother. These we must have. Still, the spiritual struggle we are in makes it adequately clear that we cannot allow anything dark into the life of the church. May God help us to find his–and only his–way out of this tension.

Col. 3:12–17

When God alone rules in every heart we will have a healthy community, full of joy, full of dedication, and full of love. Everyone will feel this in the atmosphere. Each member will go to another and ask forgiveness for where he has caused hurt or harmed love in the past. And this will be done not because someone has said it should be done but out of an inner urge.

Every church needs voices that dare to speak for Christ, even when this is painful for the person speaking as well as for other members. But speaking out must always be done in the love of Christ, otherwise it is a sin.

1 Jn. 3:8 Jesus came to earth to destroy the works of the devil, and he has millions of angels of God at his disposal to help him in this spiritual struggle. But Satan also has many angels – evil spirits, devils, and demons – at his disposal.

This spiritual struggle shows itself like this: the Holy Spirit, which is the spirit of Jesus, helps us to find God and to give us his thoughts and his love. This spirit helps us to overcome all evil and impure emotions. At the same time, the devil works in our hearts, giving us thoughts of evil, impurity, murder, envy, mistrust, and the desire for power. Yet all of us have guardian angels who will protect us if we follow what is good.

Christ must come to the deepest depths of our inner being, deeper than our conscious thoughts, deeper than our usual feelings – to the uttermost depths. Every person who knows something of deep inner struggles has an inkling of this. Through Christ he can find courage to believe against all unbelief, even where there was never any hope for belief, and strength to hope against all hope of finding love in another person.

From a letter: It is understandable that you are afraid of what others think of you. But even if it is understandable, it is a sin. When we are completely dependent on God, we will have the courage to stand up to anyone who violates our own conscience or that of anyone else, or to anyone who mistreats another. It is a sin to be silent out of fear. I have committed this sin many times in my life, but I have also seen the bitter fruit it brought to myself and to the whole church.

All of us know the struggles of the human heart, yet we have to see beyond them. We have to see the struggle of the whole church against darkness. It is an enormous struggle. And ultimately, we have to see it all in relation to the much greater struggle of the whole universe, which is led by God with his armies of thousands and thousands of angels and his stars of light, music, and harmony.

Mt. 5:13 "You are salt to the world. And if salt becomes tasteless, how is its saltiness to be restored? It is good for nothing but to be thrown away and trodden underfoot." If we are to be salt we cannot be diplomats who agree with the arguments of evil; we cannot be "fair." We must be completely and wholly one-sided in our loyalty to God and to Jesus.

From a letter: We have to make a decision for Christ,
Mt. 12:30 otherwise we will turn against him. The world situation impels us to take a stand for Christ – a stand against violence, injustice, hatred, and impurity. We must witness to this not only in words but in deeds. Our lives must prove that there is a better way.

From the Covenant of the Lord's Supper *

We declare ourselves in unity under God's judgment and mercy.

We vow that we want to live in reverence for God, for Christ, and for his Holy Spirit.

The cross, where the forgiveness of sins can be found, is the center of our life.

---

*The Covenant of the Lord's Supper was written by Heinrich Arnold and signed by all members of his church on December 30, 1975, after a year of intense struggle, to clarify the position of the brotherhood on several important issues.

We declare war against all irreverence toward God, his Christ, and his church.

We declare war against the misuse of the name of God, of Christ, and of the Holy Spirit.

We declare war against all irreverence toward the childlike spirit of Jesus as it lives in children, and we want to fight for those older children in whom the childlike spirit has been partly lost.

We declare war against all emotional or physical cruelty toward children.

We declare war against the search for power over the souls of other people, including children. We seek the atmosphere of the church and of the angels of God.

We vow to pray for the light of Jesus so that all who are in bondage or tormented by evil thoughts may be freed, and so that all those who serve darkness may be revealed and called to repentance.

We declare war against the spirit of mammon and all false love connected with mammon.

We declare war against all human greatness and all forms of vanity.

We declare war against all pride, including collective pride.

We declare war against the spirit of unforgiveness, envy, and hatred.

We vow to lay down before the cross our own power and our own "greatness."

We declare war against any degrading of others, including those who have fallen into sin.

We declare war against all cruelty to anyone, even if he has sinned.

We declare war against all forms of magic or curiosity about satanic darkness.

We ask for the courage to rejoice in suffering and persecution for the cause of right.

We ask for forgiveness of our sins, because without Jesus our hearts and our actions cannot be pure.

We pray to live for the world as Jesus expressed it in John 17: that we may all be one as Christ is one with the Father, so that the world may believe that Christ was sent by the Father. With Christ we ask not to be taken out of this world but to be protected from the power of evil.

Jn. 17:21

We ask Christ to consecrate our brotherhood through his truth. Christ's Word is the truth. We ask that he may send us out to be a light in this world.

World Suffering

1 Tm. 6:10 If we look for the roots of suffering, we will find them in possessiveness and the spirit of mammon. This
Jn. 8:44 spirit is of Satan, who is a murderer from the beginning, as Jesus said. It brings darkness and death. Many who serve it try to hide behind marvelous ideals. But despite these ideals the fruits of this spirit are injustice and death, and these are the cause of the suffering of our time and of all times. If we look at world suffering honestly, we will see how closely it is connected with our own guilt and the guilt of all men today, and we will also recognize that since this suffering is all one, we are part of it and must suffer with all others who suffer.

There is so much pain on the earth! If we are filled with God's love, we will experience this pain ourselves; we will feel something of the need of children, the elderly, the mentally disturbed, the unwanted, and the starving. But if we see only the suffering of the world, our view is completely one-sided. For God's sake we must recognize and proclaim the fact that suffering is a fruit of the great sin and guilt of the world, a fruit of man's rebellion against God.

Only God knows how much of the world's need is sin and how much of it is suffering. It has been said that if one were to put the evil of the world on one side of a scale and its suffering on the other, the scale would balance. I do not know if this is true, but it is quite clear that sin and suffering go together. War, for example, is sin, but it also involves enormous suffering. God sees both the sin and the suffering.

We believe in God's indescribable longing to save humankind not only from its need but also from its sin. It is irreverent to talk of world need without seeing the hurt done to God by world sin, which is also our sin.

If it were not for God's longing to seek men through Jesus, there would be nothing but inner and physical death on earth. Jesus is the Lamb of God who carries the sins of the world. He is the answer – the only answer to all sin and need.

When we see the world's churches as they are today, where money has so much power and there is so little compassion for the poor, we should feel challenged to reach out more. We know that the first believers in the church at Rome fed their own poor and the poor of the whole city.* They lived in the first love of Jesus,

---

*Eberhard Arnold, ed. *The Early Christians* (Rifton, NY: Plough, 1997), pp. 14–15.

and that is where we are found wanting. The hour demands that we return to this first love.

Mt. 25:31–46 *From a letter:* In Matthew 25 Jesus speaks of those who are hungry, thirsty, naked, and in prison. We, too, are concerned about these people, about the hunger and want of the world. But what should we do? We live too well. We should eat less and do with less, so as to share with the poor. The early Christians fasted for one or two days a week so as to give food to the hungry. We are not doing enough by sharing just among our own brothers and sisters. We should appoint at least one brother from each of our communities to seek out people in need, to bring them food and clothing, and to see that they have adequate heating, and so on.

From a letter: You say that the poor have no longing for God, that they are completely dull and indifferent, that you yourself have spent time in a boarding house for tramps, and that they wanted nothing else than to get to the top themselves, to oppress others, and so on. You even say that there is no point in trying to help such people–they want nothing else anyway.

Dear brother, this is not the spirit of the love of Jesus. It is true that many people are inwardly dull, but this apathy is an expression of their need. It is a sign–

probably the worst sign – of how strongly Satan, the enemy of Jesus and the murderer from the beginning, still rules over people. Don't you realize how deeply it must grieve Jesus when we talk about the need of our fellowmen in such a cold and superior way?

Do you think Jesus had this attitude? Do you believe he would have died for us if he had felt this way? We cannot talk like this about the poor and oppressed – no, we are called to love our fellowmen, and especially those who are so badly off that they can no longer see the way ahead.

From a letter: To offer a night's lodging to a homeless person has always been a fundamental principle of our church. The police have sometimes brought us homeless people, even families with children, in the middle of the night, and we have always found a way of giving them a place to sleep.

Under Hitler's regime the German secret police forbade our community to take in any guests. But we informed them that we would never refuse a night's lodging to anyone, even if the police disapproved of it; we would never close the door to a homeless person.

We would lose our whole witness if we were not even willing to give a night's lodging to a person in need. But the main thing is love. Paul says that even
1 Cor. 13:3 if we give all our possessions to the poor but have no love, it will be of no use.

In the first years of our community, whenever an unwed mother came to our house in search of a place to stay, my father would invite her for at least two or three nights. Several of these women had been thrown out of their homes, so they stayed on, and some had their babies while with us. We also had drunkards, thieves, and people who were wanted by the police. Once a murderer who had served more than twenty years in prison lived with us. My parents were not worried about the possible repercussions of exposing us children to such situations. But we were never exposed to sexual impurity. If there was indecent behavior on the part of those we took in, my father did not tolerate it.

None of these people joined us, and I don't think any of them had any interest in us as a church; they were just homeless. But my father never refused any of them a roof. The Bible says that by giving shelter to strangers, many have entertained angels without knowing it. Heb. 13:2

In these days of violent upheaval in our country, the extreme right is very active.* At the same time, others with high ideals who speak out for righteousness and justice among men and nations are also very active. We cannot stand aside. If people go to prison and give their lives for their beliefs, we can have only the

---

*Written June 13, 1964.

deepest respect and reverence for it. But we should also long and strive for a righteousness deeper than one based on human rights.

I am concerned about an incident that has occurred locally, and I don't know how we should respond.* A man from our neighborhood was beaten – struck over the head twice – because he removed anti-Semitic posters that had been displayed publicly. How should we protest such violence, and how should we witness to love and justice? On the one hand, there is a danger of getting too involved in politics; it isn't our task. On the other hand, we cannot be silent about injustice in our own neighborhood; we cannot simply be complacent and say that it isn't our business. Having lived in Germany in the 1930s, I know what it means when people are silent in such matters. Hitler was able to take over Germany only because so many people did not dare to protest or get involved.

The world is heading in a serious direction; the arms race has men preparing for mass murder such as the world has never seen. In Vietnam people are being tortured, wounded, and killed daily.† What is our responsibility? We must ask ourselves this question

* Written April 12, 1964.
† Written August 22, 1965.

quite openly. We have done very little. We have joined the marches against racial injustice in the South, and we have spoken out against the war in Vietnam. We have visited our senators and representatives to tell them of our concern, but all this is very little.

We know that the past, the present, and the future lie in God's hands, and if we give ourselves to God we must be ready to suffer and even die. Men like Michael Schwerner* died for their belief that love among men must be strengthened. We, too, should be ready to suffer and to die if God asks it of us.

Our hearts are small – I know it of myself – but we will find an answer to the question of our responsibility if we let ourselves be moved by God. Any other way will fail. If God's love moves our hearts, our lives will take on new depths and heights, and he will lead us to take the right action. But we must ask him to move our hearts today, tomorrow, and every day.

Jas. 4:17

To be complacent in the face of injustice is a terrible sin, and therefore we have great respect for the Civil Rights Movement. Many people in it are making sacrifices for righteousness, and some have even sacrificed their lives. But the fight for civil rights itself will not bring about the kingdom of God, and we must not lose sight of this, in spite of our respect for those who sacrifice everything for it. Something much greater

---

*Young civil rights activist murdered in Mississippi in 1964.

must come into being, something we ourselves cannot make: the powerful atmosphere of the spirit of Jesus, which must penetrate into all the world.

As injustice continues to increase, let us hold on to our hope in the kingdom of God and seek to live according to it, to show the world a new righteousness that includes love even to the enemy. This is the answer to the great need of our time in the world at large, but especially on the political and racial scene here in America.

Daniel and all the other prophets–as well as John in his Book of Revelation–speak of the "last days" before the kingdom of God comes, when humankind will have to face heavy judgment. The famines and pestilences of every century, the persecution of our Anabaptist forefathers and countless other small groups, the Thirty Years' War, and the wiping out of Native Americans are all examples of enormous suffering that already fulfill many prophecies of judgment. So are the First and Second World Wars, which held perhaps the greatest horrors humankind has ever seen. The last days have already begun.

There is such endless need on earth – much more than we can ever know. Some of it is economic need, and some of it is social need, but in a deeper way it is all inner need brought into men's lives by the dark powers of injustice, murder, and unfaithfulness. Some of us used to believe that through political or social measures radical changes could take place in our society – changes that would answer this need. But as we have seen again and again, the leaders of today's world always get caught in their own lies and webs of dishonesty; the cold dollar rules, and impurity and unfaithfulness are everywhere.

We know that our few communities will not change the world. But Christ will, and we want to give ourselves voluntarily to him. He demands our whole personality and our whole life. He came to save the world, and we believe that he, not any human leader, will one day govern the earth. For him we live and give our utmost, and for him we are willing to die.

Mission

It is our deep longing as a brotherhood that we may reach out to other seeking people. But this does not mean that we should all drive off and talk to people about our faith. Mission has to be given by God in a burning, genuine way so that we are led to those who want to hear. We cannot just preach to people. We seek an inner, personal relationship with them – something that cannot be made by men. Only God can give us the right word at the right time for the right person.

We are not interested in attracting members, as people sometimes think. Our movement would collapse if
cf. Mt. 12:30 that were our motive. We want to gather because
cf. Mt. 23:37 Jesus tells us to gather. When my brother Hardy was studying at Tübingen University in the 1930s, my father asked him to arrange some public lectures there. Hardy had large posters put up, announcing that Dr. Eberhard Arnold would speak about his community. But my father said, "I certainly won't do that. I will speak about God's cause. I won't mention our community." The cause of God should be our main concern.

We long to have contact with more people, but all our wishes and longings must come under one desire: that at any hour, in any place, not our will but God's will be done. We must willingly submit to this. The last few years have shown us – or should have shown us – our incapability, our sinfulness, and our powerlessness. Mission depends on whether our faith is a living faith.

Let us watch that we do not go out on mission in human strength. There is enough preaching in the world; so many people go out of their own accord and preach. I am all for mission, but only if it is God's will that moves us, and not our own egos.

In the early church, where true mission was alive in a special way, there were two important conditions: the believers were of one heart, mind, and soul, and they were repentant. We must find this oneness of heart, mind, and soul, and we must find the humility and repentance of Paul.

We cannot escape the command of mission. For a church to remain alive, missionaries must be sent out, two by two perhaps, as in the early church or among the Anabaptists of the 16th century. The city must stand on a hill, and the light must shine out. Does the world really recognize through today's church that the Father sent Jesus Christ into the world? Do we not have an enormous responsibility? Jesus' last words to
Mk. 16:15–18 his disciples were, "Go into all the world and preach the good news to all creation. Whoever believes and is

baptized will be saved, but whoever does not believe will be condemned."

It is unlikely that there will be another Pentecost where thousands are baptized in one day. But we long that the seeds of Jesus might be planted in our corrupt society, even if we must leave it to God whether the seeds become plants and bear fruit. The twelve apostles accomplished much, but they were sent with the authority of Christ. Nothing like it has happened again since.

I know mission cannot be forced, but I have an enormous longing that the seed is sown, that men awaken and love Jesus and keep his words. Then he will come to them and dwell with them.

Let us pray that whenever we mention the name of the Lord and proclaim the Gospel, it is with the fire of the Holy Spirit. That is the need of our age, the need of our poor earth, which was visited by the Son of God and has not been forgotten by him.

The cross is deeply implanted into the earth. It points to heaven, but its outstretched arms express the hunger and thirst of Jesus for all men. Christ said, "I shall draw all men to myself when I am lifted up from the earth." (Jn. 12:32)

Our life seems to have a certain contradiction. On the one hand, we would like to embrace the whole of humankind. If it were possible, we would like to convince thousands and millions of people to live as brothers and sisters in Christ. We want as many as possible to come to us so we can share with them. And we long that our missionary urge might grow even stronger. On the other hand, we would rather have only two or three members who are wholly dedicated, than hundreds and hundreds of people who are not. We do not want the salt of our witness to be lost. We would rather be a group of only a few, with real love and real faith in Christ, than a mass movement where there is hatred and jealousy.

According to the first three Gospels, the twelve
Mt. 28:19–20 apostles were sent on mission with the words, "Go out
Mk. 16:15–18 into all the world and make disciples of all nations,
Lk. 24:47 and baptize them in the name of the Father, the Son,
and the Holy Spirit." In the Gospel of John, Jesus
Jn. 17:21 speaks of another form of mission: "May they all be
one, Father, as thou art in me and I in thee. May they
also be one in us so that the world may believe that
thou hast sent me."

This is so important for us today. Here Jesus does not put the emphasis on preaching the Gospel to win people from the world, but on unity: "May they all be one, so that the world will believe that thou hast sent me." In this prayer, mission consists in the unity of the disciples.

Unity costs a fight; it costs church discipline and suffering; it costs renewed forgiveness, trust, and love over and over to the same people who have hurt us. If unity is strong among us, it will shine out into the world. We do not know how, but it will.

We must long for more and more love to stream out from our circle so that we can send people out on mission from a united church. Until we can do this we are not yet living for love alone. When we do not have the strength for mission, it is a sign that our church is not fully dedicated to love, and this should humble us.

We live in community because we want to be brothers and sisters. That is our first calling: to be brothers, also to the humblest people, so that no one is looked down upon and no one's need is forgotten. We are here to take care of our children, our brothers and sisters, our old people, widows, and orphans. It is not our main calling to seek out people from the slums and the like; that could even destroy us. If everyone were to scatter, things would go to pieces and we would become like any other organization set up to do social work.

If we look at our discipleship in the light of Jesus' words about raising the dead and casting out devils, we will see that we are a very poor church spiritually. This should make us humble, but it should not make us resigned.

Mt. 10:8
Mk. 16:15–18

In my father's last letter he wrote, "We have not yet arrived at true mission, but it is more and more urgent to pray for it." I know he hoped for this kind of mission – raising the dead and casting out demons – to be given again in our time. It was not important to him whether it would be given to him personally or to our church, but that it would be given *somewhere*.

From a letter: I long for apostolic mission – to go to the roadsides and fences and invite men to the great festival of the kingdom of God. But every day lived in true unity is mission too. Read John 17, where Jesus says that by the unity and love of the disciples the world will recognize that the Father sent him. There is no greater vision than that. If only we fight our way through to this unity, God will give us the strength to carry out both forms of mission, and every member will take part.

Jn. 17:21

From a letter: The sharpness of Jesus as a part of the Gospel is no longer preached in Christendom today. John the Baptist began his message with the words,

Mt. 3:7–9 "You generation of vipers! Who told you that you could escape the judgment that is to come? Then show the fruits that are in accord with a change of heart! And don't think you can get anywhere by thinking, 'Abraham is our father.'"

I consider it my inner calling and duty to proclaim the Gospel with the same sharpness, though also with the same kindness and compassion that is found in the New Testament.

Lk. 10:3 Jesus sent out his apostles under the sign of the lamb. Anyone who has been put under pressure, especially religious pressure, will know why he did this. It becomes even clearer if one thinks of the dove, which is the symbol of the spirit of God. Its nature is trusting and innocent, without any force, pressure, or evil, unable to attack or override another's free will. The Spirit came upon Jesus like a dove. This is the character of apostolic mission: no coercion, no pressure, no persuasion. The stronger personality must never override the weaker; it must be harmless as a dove. Yet
Mt. 10:16 along with Jesus' words, "Be innocent as doves," he says, "Be wise as serpents."

In our corrupt time it is the responsibility of the church to call men to a life in God and in Jesus. If we look at society today, we can see that humankind is wholly corrupt; it is not at all reconciled with God.

Reconciliation with God is possible only through the cross. Without Jesus and his suffering and death, no one can find God.

Many of us long for our church to carry out apostolic mission, and I am thankful that this longing is alive. But unless we are sent by God as Paul was sent we will never be able to do mission, even in a humbler form. At the time of Paul's conversion Jesus told him,

Acts 26:18

"I send you to open men's eyes and turn them from darkness to light, and from the dominion of Satan to God, so that by trust in me they may obtain forgiveness of sins and a place with those whom God has made his own." That is the purpose of mission. It is clear that mission can never be a human undertaking. We are incapable of it – absolutely incapable – without a deep inner relationship to God, to Jesus, and to the church.

With regard to participating in today's various movements of social protest, I hope we are given the sensitivity both to recognize what is God-given and encourage it, and to reject what is not good. We must be open to receive, but at the same time we must witness to true brotherhood.

The Kingdom of God

Jesus

Jesus was the suffering servant. His life went from birth in a lowly stable to death on a cross between two criminals for the sake of pure love alone. He was a true man, yet God; he was the Word that became flesh; he was the Son of God but also called himself the Son of Man.

Jesus Christ is the redeemer who comes to us weak and sinful men. He frees us from sin and demonic powers. He makes us true men. He is the healer who heals for nothing. He is the true vine, the living tree. He is the same yesterday, today, and in all eternity. Jesus is the soul of compassion, the friend of man, the caller to new life. He is the true and good shepherd, the king of God's kingdom. He is called the wonderful counselor, mighty God, everlasting Father, and prince of peace.

Christ is the gathering power: "How often have I
Lk. 13:34 wanted to gather you like a hen her chicks, and you
Jn. 17:21 would not." His last prayer was for unity and love among his disciples. His new life overcomes separation, leads to community, and makes men of one heart and one soul. He is the revelation of God's love and kingdom.

We must experience Jesus in our hearts and souls. Yet still more is demanded: we must experience him as Lord over all things, king over all principalities and worlds of God. We must concentrate our hearts, minds, and souls on the vision of his kingdom and on him, the coming one.

From a letter: I know you have difficulties with certain biblical concepts of Christ. But if you do not want the whole Christ, even the part that you do accept will slip through your fingers, and you will be left with nothing. I lay this on your heart with love and concern.

Lk. 1:26–38 Ultimately, it is a question of whether you accept Jesus Christ, who was born of the virgin Mary through the Holy Spirit. All power in heaven and on earth is

Col. 1:20 given to him, and he came into this world to reconcile the whole universe to himself, making peace through the shedding of his blood upon the cross.

Faith in Christ means the willingness to believe in mysteries that we can neither see, feel, nor understand with our stupid intellect.

I often wonder whether we have the whole Christ sufficiently in mind. For any Christian–for individuals as well as for churches–there is a danger of experiencing only a part of Christ–accepting only a part of his message–and being faithful to that. We must find and serve the whole Christ. I am not able to proclaim, "Here, this is the whole Christ." Even if we learned the entire Gospel by heart, we could not say we have the whole Christ. Only the Holy Spirit is able to bring him to us.

Jesus sees the evil in a person so sharply and clearly that it is as if he had no love; yet he sees hope for a person so strongly that it is as if there were no evil in him. In the New Testament we find the sharpest words of eternal condemnation and, at the same time, the most tender love.

We have to love everything in Jesus – his sharpness and his compassion. If we love his sharpness, then our hearts will be purified and pruned; but we could not live if his love, compassion, and mercy were not still greater.

It is a mistake to think that Jesus was only brave and
2 Cor. 13:4 strong. He was crucified in weakness, and that is a deep mystery. He became weak for our sake, for the sins of the world, and to bring reconciliation and the victory of God into earth and heaven. This is why we love him.

Jesus was crucified in weakness, but he now lives in the power of God. We, too, are weak, as he was, yet through God's power we can become one with him and full of life.

If we are proud we cannot live through God's power, for when we are strong and great in spirit, we stand in his way. But if we are weak, that is no hindrance.

Jn. 15:1–17

In John 15, Jesus speaks from the depth of his heart about the unity of his followers. He speaks of himself as a vine and his Father as a vine-dresser who cuts away every branch that fails to bear fruit and prunes those that bear fruit so that they may bear still more.

The Savior does not cut us off completely to wither away; rather, he cleanses us and binds us afresh to his vine. We must undergo this experience of punishment and judgment, for Jesus says that whoever bears fruit, he cleanses. When a vinedresser cleans branches, he uses a knife. We must pray that the knife may cut deeply into our hearts, no matter how much it hurts, so that cleansed by him we may be grafted to the one vine.

Jn. 15:4, 7

Our Savior says, "Dwell in me, and I shall dwell in you." I have the deep longing that we all may dwell in him, and he in us. There is nothing greater, nothing more wonderful, nothing more joyful than unity with Jesus Christ.

The angel that appeared to the shepherds said, "Unto

Lk. 2:11

you a child is born. Unto you a son is given." We must take that to heart: *to you* a child is born. It is not just a matter of believing that a child is born in Bethlehem, but that a child is born *to you*. We must believe this quite personally: Jesus came for each of us.

Jesus' life began in a stable and ended on the cross
between two criminals. The Apostle Paul said he
1 Cor. 2:2 wanted to proclaim nothing but this crucified Christ.
We, too, have nothing to hold to except this Christ.
We must ask ourselves again and again: Are we willing
2 Tm. 3:12 to go his way, from the stable to the cross? As disciples
we are not promised comfortable and good times.
Jesus says we must deny ourselves and suffer with him
and for him. That is the only way to follow him, but
behind it lies the glory of life – the glowing love of
God, which is so much greater than our hearts and
our lives.

From a letter: Jesus was a strong man in a new way.
He was at once very weak and very strong. He was
Mt. 23:37 not ashamed to shed tears over Jerusalem, whom he
wanted to gather like a hen her chicks; he was not
Jn. 11:35 afraid to weep publicly at the raising of Lazarus; and
he was not afraid to show his agony in Gethsemane.
All this did not make for a "strong" man in the worldly
sense. Yet Jesus' love was so strong that he was able to
Lk. 22:44 suffer the most terrible pain and godforsakenness, and
in this strength he completed the task given him by his
Father.

In true weakness we become powerless, and in true powerlessness we find strength. That is the secret.

Each of us must have a personal relationship to Jesus. As a young man, I could not understand why the feeling of joy and love I had in the first weeks after my conversion did not last. I was very troubled and asked my father about it. He said, "You can't base your Christianity on feelings. There are times when one simply has to follow without deep feelings."

Eph. 5:22–33 Paul compares the relationship of Christ and his church to marriage, which sometimes brings joy, and sometimes sorrow. The main thing is faithfulness to the relationship; one's feelings will not always be the same. When we are called back to the first love, it can give us a tremendous feeling of joy, which is a gift from God. This feeling will not last a lifetime. But if we are faithful, our relationship with Christ will remain even when we go through times of pain and tears, sorrow and emptiness.

Jn. 14:23 Jesus says, "He who loves me heeds what I say, and I will come with the Father and dwell in him." There is nothing more intimate than dwelling in another's heart.

Jn. 6:53–56 Jesus also says, "He who does not drink my blood and eat my flesh cannot belong to me." It is a Gospel of complete oneness; it excludes the possibility of
Rv. 3:15 half-heartedness. Jesus prefers the ice-cold heart to the lukewarm.

If we love someone, we want to know his innermost being. We are not satisfied with simply knowing him outwardly. So it is with our love to God. If we give ourselves to him, we will learn to know his innermost being and heart, his character and his love. It is not enough just to speak of God. We seek his revelation.
Heb. 12:6 The Bible says that those whom God loves he chastises. So we should thank God if we are punished and chastised, for it is a sign of his love. We cannot experience the complete liberation brought about by the forgiveness of sins if we do not accept Jesus' sharpness. Only then will we also be able to experience his goodness, his compassion, and his ultimate love.

There is a certain subjectivity in man's relationship with Jesus that we reject because it forgets the greatness of God and the church – as if only *my* soul and *my* salvation were important. But to reject one's inner relationship to Jesus as subjective in itself would be wrong. We do have to experience his love, his death on the cross, and his forgiveness in a personal way.

Everything we need in order to find God is given to us in Christ. But it does not help to grasp that with our brains. Nor does it help to learn the Bible or recite prayers by heart. Jesus must touch our hearts to the depths so that we are moved by his person.
Jn. 6:53–59 He compares this experience to eating his flesh and

drinking his blood. That is the opposite of a merely intellectual experience. It is an experience from the depths of the heart.

True discipleship demands that we love Jesus so deeply that all other love – even our love to wife and children – is small in comparison. We must love him so much that even the smallest part of his Gospel is of greatest importance to us. We must love everything in him: his death, his resurrection, his judgment, and his future eternal kingdom. But most of all we must love his inner life, insofar as he has revealed it to us in his life and death. This inner life is the spirit of God. The greatest task of a Christian is to love Jesus, to recognize him, and to learn to understand him in his innermost being.

Jesus wants us to love everything in him – his deeds, his parables, his rejection of mammon and worldly goods, his pureness of heart and faithfulness in relationships, his sorrow and suffering over injustice, his death with criminals – but most of all *him* personally, his heart and his blood.

The Jews found it very hard to accept the idea of drinking Jesus' blood and eating his flesh, for it was forbidden by the law of Moses to drink blood. But Jesus wanted to show his disciples a unity and community which he could compare only with flesh and blood. He is actually speaking about eternal community with him in the kingdom of God.

Mt. 9:12 Jesus came as a physician for the sick and a shepherd
Jn. 10:14–15 for the lost – not only for the just and righteous. He is God's love at work on earth. If we really understand this, we will realize that following Jesus means suffering. It cannot be a comfortable way.

From a letter: Dedicate yourself daily to the person of Jesus. Then it will be possible to burn for him and to give up all self-concern.

When Jesus lived on earth, he promised that he would come again to found the kingdom of God, a kingdom of peace and love. In the parable of the ten virgins, five
Mt. 25:1–13 of them were ready, but five had no oil – no burning love to God and men. Even though the five foolish ones had the outer form of the lamp, their inner fire was gone. Jesus said he did not know them, and they could not take part in the kingdom.

This parable speaks to our time, because it is almost two thousand years since Jesus lived on earth, and we have gotten used to waiting. The world goes on as before. But the time will come when we will wish we had oil.

Lk. 14:33

If we want to be disciples of Christ we must be prepared to bear everything in faith and give up everything as he did. The total surrender of the crucified Christ must be proclaimed over and over again in the church to every new generation.

From a letter: I thank God that you feel an inkling of the reality of Jesus in your life. Nourish this small flame and let it grow. Jesus can come into your heart only insofar as it is emptied of other things. If a bucket of water is full, you cannot add to it; but if it is emptied, it can be refilled. You must become empty. Jesus will touch you even if there is only a little room for him.

From a letter: Never forget that your heart must be empty and poor in spirit for Jesus to rule in it–no hidden corners can be kept for yourself. See everything from Jesus' outlook and not from your point of view. What you think and feel is not important. It is Jesus' will that is important. When you submit to him, all your feelings will change.

From a letter: If you really want to serve Jesus alone, show this in practical ways: in the way you bring up your children, in your attitude to your husband, and in your attitude to the church. It is not true that you are

a poor person, as you write. I wish you were, for Jesus
Mt. 5:3 says, "Blessed are the poor in spirit." You are sometimes very rich, rich in opinions and full of self-recognition and self-esteem. Become a poor person *in truth.*

From a letter: I know God has given you a loving heart, but your old nature must die so that you can receive his love. Then he can use you as he made you. Dying with Christ does not mean being extinguished. But it does mean pouring out our innermost being before him, bringing our sins to the cross, and becoming one with him who died for us.

Jn. 12:24 When a grain of wheat is laid in the earth, it dies. It no longer remains a grain, but through death it brings forth fruit. This is the way of true Christianity. It is the way Jesus went when he died on the cross for each of us. If we want our lives to be fruits of Christ's death on the cross, we cannot remain individual grains. We must be ready to die too.

Have Christ before you in everything so that you are able to die for him! Long to come nearer to him. Live in one spirit – in service to him – so that the grace of God may always be with you. Then, even when the day comes that your blood must be shed for him, you will be joyful. It will be nothing but victory!

Jn. 14:21 Jesus says that if we love him and fulfill his commandments, he will love us and disclose himself to us. This is not a question of a theology or a teaching but a question of life, of receiving Jesus as a real person, as the Son of Man who wants to love us and reveal himself to us. When we dwell in Jesus, he will dwell in us, and
Gal. 2:20 we can say like Paul the Apostle, "I live, yet not I, but Christ liveth in me."

The way God sent his Son into the world is not to
Jn. 1:14 be explained or understood. John simply says that the Word became flesh. This Word is his love, and he poured it out through the Holy Spirit in Mary. Only in this sense can we begin to understand the mystery of the virgin birth.

It is our prayer that we may see the real Christ. We pray that he be revealed to us first as he was – a baby born in a stable at Bethlehem; and then a condemned man hanging on the cross between two criminals at Golgotha; as he is today – the head of all things,
Eph. 5:23 especially of his church; and as he will be at the end of time – the one who judges the quick and the dead, the bridegroom of the great festival in the kingdom of God.

Are we willing to go the same way of suffering that Jesus went on earth? Are we willing to give ourselves so completely to him that we are ready to be persecuted, beaten, or even killed for his sake?

If we experience the heart of Christ, we experience something of the throne of God, which is over the whole universe, the universe that scientists can only reckon in light-years, in distances that we cannot imagine.

Heb. 1:1–3

Christ is the revelation of God. The revelation of God is always and eternally the life of Christ. God lived in him in his fullness. Christ died for us, Christ rose for us, and Christ wants to come to us. He *is* what he teaches. He reveals the source that he really is. Here is springing water for thirsty souls.

Jesus Christ! He must remain the center at all times. The church cannot be our center, for a body without a head is dead. We need constant renewal from within, and by that I mean that we need new encounters with God and Christ again and again. This must happen in communal worship meetings as well as in each individual heart. Rebirth means the indwelling of the Father, and it takes place through the Holy Spirit.

The Living Word

Jn. 1:1–3 In John 1 we read, "In the beginning was the Word. Before all things were made, there was the Word." What is this word? A human word spoken from one person to another, a sincere word of love, first belongs to the one who speaks it. It lives in a person, it burns in him, and then it is spoken into the heart of another. But now we are speaking of God's Word – the living Word. This Word, this personal expression of God, was in the beginning with God and all things were made through him, and without him nothing was made. It is so powerful, it cannot be printed or written down. That will be the kingdom of God – when he speaks his Word into people's hearts, when he judges them and they agonize over the injustice and wickedness, the lying, murder and discord, the impurity of this earth. cf. Rv. 19:11–16

This Word became flesh and dwelt among us. It happened in the town of Bethlehem. The Word really became a human being, but he was and is the anointed God, the Christ.

2 Pt. 1:19 Like the sun, Christ rises in a believing heart. "He is the morning star and the sun of the believing heart." This inner light alone can overcome the darkness in us.

---

*In this chapter, Arnold draws heavily on the thoughts of his father, Eberhard Arnold, specifically using the last chapter of his book, *Innerland*, entitled, "The Living Word."

Some people are tormented by inner confusion. Christ
came into this darkness. He transforms the whole
earth. His Word enters the hearts of dying men to
Dt. 6:6 change them from the bottom up. "Take to heart the
words I speak to you today." That means Jesus speaks
now, to *you* – that is the living Word. As soon as your
inner life is set on fire, his Word awakens new growth.

Nothing at all can help us – nothing except the Word
of God. By the Word we do not mean the mere letters
of the Bible. It is true that since the Bible contains the
sayings of Jesus and the prophets in written form, it is
the holiest book that exists. But the Bible itself is not
the Word, it only witnesses to it. When we read the
Bible and feel God speaking directly into our hearts,
when our hearts start to burn, we know it is the living
2 Cor. 3:6 Word. "The dead letter kills, but the Spirit brings life."
When the Word penetrates our hearts we experience
how Jesus lived, how he died, why he died, and how
he rose and ascended into heaven. Christ himself is the
essence of scripture.

The Bible itself is *not* the Word of God. You are not
proclaiming the Word of God simply by reading
aloud from the Bible. When Jesus was tempted in the
Mt. 4:4 wilderness, he said to the tempter, "Man does not live
by bread alone, but by every word that comes from

the mouth of God." It is by this living Word that comes from the mouth of God that Jesus drove away the tempter. The living Word is what God speaks to you now, at this moment, into your heart. It is not what he said to Moses or Elijah or even to Jesus, but what he speaks to *you.* But the remarkable thing is that when God speaks to you, he never contradicts Jesus or his prophets.

Mt. 4:6 The devil knows how to use the Bible to kill souls. The Old and New Testaments will be the weapon of the Antichrist. He always comes with the Bible in hand. When the religious authorities persecuted the Anabaptist believers of Reformation times, they came with their Bibles to drown burn, behead, or hang them.

What matters is not that every word of Jesus in the New Testament is memorized but that his words are burned into our hearts by God himself. That is the
Lk. 24:32 living Word. Our prayer and proclamation should not be what I feel or think–that's why I hardly dare lead prayers in public. It should be the Word that proceeds from the mouth of God. *That* is the Gospel. We have
Mt. 4:4 to wait for Jesus to come into our hearts through God's mouth and the Holy Spirit.

Are we willing to hear God's Word, which cuts more keenly than a two-edged sword? In Hebrews it says,

Heb. 4:12–13

> The word of God is living and active, sharper than any two-edged sword, piercing to the division of soul and of spirit, of joints and of marrow, and discerning the thoughts and intentions of the heart. And no creature is hidden from his sight, but all are naked and exposed to the eyes of him to whom we must give account.

Heb. 4:15–16 But then it also says Jesus sympathizes with our weakness, fears, and inner need – he understands. If we are willing to give our hearts to this sharp sword, we will find this Jesus, the one who knows our need. But if we reject him, we will also be rejected.

Mt. 4:4 Jesus says that man does not live by bread alone but by every word that comes from the mouth of God. We do not have a silent God. The Word is not rigid, as if cast in iron into one form or contained in a book – not even when that book is the Bible. The Word never
Mt. 5:17–20 contradicts the prophets of the Old Testament, nor does it contradict the New Testament, but it is spoken over and over again anew into our hearts. Suddenly, new connections are seen and different passages light up. The Word continually reveals new insights and makes everything alive for us. We cannot exist without the living Word of God, and we have to testify to this.

From a letter: I rejoice that the Bible has become alive for you. That is so important: not the letter but the living Jesus. May he burn in our hearts and lives. Then we will no longer be so concerned with our outer activities that our inner life suffers. When Jesus is the center of our lives, our inner life will become like a flame that burns for him.

The Word does not help us as long as it remains outside our hearts. It has to enter into us. This is the only way to become free of dark powers. The crucified
1 Pt. 1:18–21 Christ penetrating our hearts is the essence of scripture and the witness of Christ's disciples. Christ alone is the
1 Jn. 4:1–3 scale on which spirits can be weighed.

Jn. 1:1 Christ was the Word before everything began, a long time before the Bible was ever written. You cannot put God in bookstores and sell him for twenty dollars apiece. But certainly when God speaks in our hearts, he never contradicts the words of Jesus. "The Holy
Jn. 14:26 Spirit will remind you of every word that I have said to you." And that happens. Every Christian experiences it many times. So let us ask God to give us a living church – never dead rules, or dead laws. I wish so much for a fresh wind to blow so that everything cold and old and of the "law" is swept away by this living wind of God.

If we are in deep inner need – in spiritual darkness – then we will find healing only by accepting the living Word of Jesus. If his Word is to heal, it must come directly from his heart and enter our heart and soul. Then the open book of the Bible suddenly becomes
Heb. 4:12–14 a flaming book. Every letter is like fire. Christ comes into the heart as fire and hot coals – it can be compared to tasting salt, it is so real.

To proclaim the Word, it's not enough to go to
Acts 4:13–14 university or attend seminary; that is not even needed. What is necessary is to be a lowly person, and to live from the heart. When we do this, our human theories and theology and the world of our own thoughts will fall away, and Jesus himself will come to us and give us his healing medicine; we receive him in person.

There are plenty of places in the Bible where two passages apparently contradict each other. Both must contain truth, for God deceives no one. If we listen to the Spirit deep down, we will understand. If we listen to our intellect only, we remain far from the truth of
1 Cor. 2:10–16 God. The Bible is closed to the scholarly approach. Only the master has the key to this book. He is the truth, who was from the beginning with God and who became flesh. He is the source of understanding and he is life. Without Christ himself no one can understand the truth.

What matters is that you experience Jesus through his Spirit in your heart. It is not enough to read the New Testament or the prophets. It has to be an experience deep in the heart, in the innermost center of a person. This does not go without feeling judged, but it should always lead to the certainty that Jesus forgives and accepts you.

When Christ speaks directly into our hearts, it is always a sign of his love. The love of Christ judges us. For this reason we should read the Bible, especially the New Testament, again and again. When God himself speaks to us, we are freed from our self-will, cold-heartedness, and self-importance. Our arrogance dies. We are challenged to turn away from ourselves and turn to the eternal light, to Christ. The Word leads to unity with Christ and unity with the heart of God. There is nothing more moving than this great, moved heart of God. People inclined to center around themselves and their own complexities completely forget the heart of God.

When a person is touched by the heart of God – the living Word – preoccupation with self disappears. He becomes united with Christ, so united that he will want to follow Christ completely, even to the cross.
Phil. 3:7–11 These are not mere words. Believers throughout the ages suffered torture, and were beheaded, burned alive,

hanged, or drowned for the sake of Christ. We do not have to go back very far: this is happening even today.

The light of Christ shines in every person who keeps his eyes on the cross – the suffering of the cross. At the cross the Word comes alive: suddenly God speaks to us. What an everlastingly good and compassionate God he is! No one can feel this love of God or know his truth if filled with worldly lusts. The Holy Spirit brings us Christ, the crucified. I long for this Spirit.

Eph. 3:14–19 When the crucified Christ penetrates deeply into
our hearts we will understand the enormous goodness
Jn. 17:20–23 and mercy of God. We will feel deeply united with
all who have given their lives to this same Christ. No dead dogma; only the living Word! Christ, living in our hearts. In absolute trust in Jesus, every difficult question is answered – even for a world that has gone to pieces.

A person sometimes grapples with a problem and only finds the answer with the living Word; that is, by God himself speaking into his heart – not his intellect. I have experienced this personally in struggling with the question of salvation.

When I encountered Christ, he came to me in an overwhelming way, and I felt flooded with a love for all people. This happened three times in my life, and each time it was as if I had been thrown to the ground. Each time I was overcome with love for all people.

Now if you read certain verses of the Bible, you could conclude that only very few people will be saved, and that most will be damned. If you are filled with love for all human beings, this is a very terrible thought. I know some Christians really believe this. I myself find it hard to accept. On the other hand, there is the danger of thinking you are more loving than God, and hoping that God will become as loving.

I have struggled long and hard over this question. At sixty, I have never known hatred to be part of an encounter with God, which is why I have such trouble with the thought that most people are born to be damned – even if it could be proved as "biblical" by reading the Bible too literally. So what is the answer? To me, it lies in recognizing that the Bible itself is not the living Word, but only a witness to it. The Word of God can only be spoken into your heart by God himself.

If we want to be like Jesus – and every person should
1 Jn. 2:6 try to be like him – we must be willing to carry his
Mk. 10:39 cross. Then the Word will become truth in our hearts.
When we meet God, we will quake, as Mary did when
the angel appeared to her. We have to be willing for
the pain, inner poverty, and inner suffering of birth to
Lk. 1:26–38 receive new life. When this Word is born, and becomes
flesh, it radiates love, and wants to live in God, *only*

God. When the Word is born in us, we no longer desire darkness. We are awakened by Christ. We are liberated from our hells. We become a brother of Jesus,
Mt. 12:50 a sister of Jesus, and a mother of Jesus. "Those who do the will of my Father are my mother, my sisters, and my brothers." *We* become that church of Jesus Christ. Now we can proclaim that Christ indeed became flesh. It is not an intellectual concept, it is life-changing.

Jesus is the great physician. A physician can only help someone who follows his instructions. A sick person must do what the physician says – the word he speaks at the moment. Above all, a patient must stop trying to cure himself with his own ideas or with other people's advice.

Ex. 15:26 God said: "I, the Lord, am your physician." God's medicine has to be taken internally; externally it does no good. If you are coughing and the doctor prescribes medicine, saying, "Take three teaspoons every three hours," and you don't follow instructions, the medicine will not help. It is far more serious if Jesus prescribes medicine and a person still thinks he knows better.

The medicine of Jesus heals completely. His healing is his presence. He himself is the medicine. We must drink the words he speaks to us. Jesus even goes so far
Jn. 6:53–59 as to say to his disciples, "Unless you eat my flesh and drink my blood you have no life in me."

I believe that a power came from Jesus that made it possible for his disciples to bear these words. It was

strictly forbidden for a Jew to drink blood – the one Jew who could say these hard words was Jesus himself. Such strong and salty language could be accepted only by men willing to pay the full price. The disciples, who had experienced the power of the living Word, would not leave Jesus. When he asked them, "Do you, too,
Jn. 6:68 want to go now?" Peter answered, "Where should we go? You have words of eternal life."

The power of the living Word liberates us from the
Jn. 8:31–36 dead letter of the law. It builds joyful, living faith. This joyful, living faith generates obedience to God,
Rom. 10:8 free from slavery to the letter. Only love rules. Love is
Dt. 30:14 freedom. "The Word is near you, on your lips and in your heart." Every individual must decide whether he wants to merely read the Bible, or receive it as a living seed in his heart.

The eyes of Christ look into our chaos and the destruction of our hearts. He will be victorious in our struggles. If we see his eyes, we sense the creative love of God that makes everything new. Jesus is God speaking; Christ is the living Word from the heart of God. The fire of God's Word is his love. If we receive
Mk. 10:30 Christ in our hearts, we experience the unbelievable joy of the Holy Spirit, of unity with brothers and sisters. The church lives in jubilation with the creative, living Word that gives all honor to Christ.

What's the use of looking at water in a well, if we do not drink? What use is the Word of God or the Bible – even if we memorize every word – if it doesn't penetrate the depths of our hearts? The Word is like living water, and living water flows into every root. The same is true of the human body and true of the
Jn. 4:13–14 church. Therefore Jesus said: "I give living water. Whoever drinks the water I give him will never be thirsty in all eternity. The water I give will be a source that continues to stream throughout eternal life."

The Cross

The fact that Jesus' blood was shed for the forgiveness of sins is a mystery. Many people say, "God is so great, so mighty, that he could have saved humankind without the cross." But that is not true. We should remember that God is not only one hundred percent love–which might have allowed him to forgive our sins without the cross. He is also one hundred percent justice. God's love and God's justice had to be revealed to the world of angels, because there are evil angels as well as holy angels.

To kill the Son of God was the most evil deed ever done. But it was just through that deed that God showed his greatest love and gave everyone the possibility of finding peace with him and the forgiveness of sins.

From a letter: We constantly need the crucified Christ within us. To receive him we must become silent before God again and again. Christ wants to live in our hearts so that we are able to conquer all things. Through him everything receives its true meaning. There is no other foundation for true peace of heart than unity with him. Only Christ can bring us to full trust in God. In him we find the sharpest judgment of wrath over all evil, but also the revelation of his loving grace.

If we do not believe in the power of evil, we cannot fully understand Jesus. It cannot be denied that he came to save men. But unless we understand that the main reason for his coming was to join the fight between God and Satan – to destroy the works of Satan – we cannot fully understand the need for an atonement-death on the cross.

1 Jn. 3:7–10

The thought that God is all-loving can insulate us from the power of his touch. People know that God forgives sin, but they forget that he judges it too. There is something in modern thinking which rebels against the atonement. Perhaps our idea of an all-loving God keeps us from wanting to face judgment. We think that love and forgiveness is all that is needed, yet that is not the whole Gospel – it makes God too human.

1 Cor. 1:18–25

It is of crucial importance that the cross of Jesus Christ is in the center of our hearts – central to our calling, and central to our mission. The Lamb of God on the cross stands before the throne of God. The cross is the center of the universe. We must experience its meaning in its height, depth, and breadth as a mystical revelation through the Holy Spirit. It is not enough to believe it; we must ask God that we may be allowed to experience it in a living way.

Rv. 5:6

Heb. 9:14

The cross is the only place where we can find purification – not only from sexual impurity, but from anything which defiles the soul: deceit, murder, hypocrisy, lovelessness, and envy. We can find purification only if we find the crucified one.

From a letter: To have the cross as the center of our lives means to love nothing more than the cross – when we get up in the morning, throughout the day, and in every situation. At a wedding two people promise to love one another until death parts them. But our love to the cross must go through death into eternal life.

If a man is confronted by a criminal, he will either judge him or show him mercy. Only God can do both in the same moment: judge him and flood him with compassion and mercy.

If we desire help in our distress – and we do experience distress – we should not cry to God first about our own suffering; we should go back in our minds and hearts to where the suffering of the world began. If we come before God with only our own inner burdens, we do him an injustice. But if we see how God has suffered since Adam's fall – especially through Christ's death on the cross – then we can ask him to free us from our own distress.

Jesus came to destroy the works of the devil, and sickness and death are works of the devil. God allows them, but in Christ he also takes them upon himself.

Mt. 26:39

Christ's seven last words begin with "My Father, if it is possible, let this cup pass me by. Yet not as I will, but as you will." We cannot imagine all that was in that cup. But he was ready to accept it, and although he did not feel God's nearness, he still gave his spirit into the hands of the Father. That is the only way to overcome the works of the devil.

When I think of Jesus, I see his cross rooted in the earth, towering to the heights, with arms stretched wide to embrace all who come to him. The cross is the only place where there is complete victory over temptation, sin, and the devil. There is no other place.

God wants to reveal the greatness of the cross to us. We all know about the cross and its meaning; we all believe in it; we are probably all moved by it; but I believe God wants it to cut like a sword through our hearts. I don't think any one of us can imagine what it means that Christ experienced godforsakenness so that we might find forgiveness of sin and eternal life in God.

We must pray for all obstacles in our hearts to be overcome so that we may experience the death of Jesus in its entirety. We are not yet moved enough by his innocent suffering and death on the cross. Jesus gave his blood so that every repentant heart might receive forgiveness of sins. His arms are wide open, as they were on the cross, for all repentant believers.

We know that many things depend on our will, and yet we know we are unable to bring ourselves to a rebirth of the Holy Spirit such as the people experienced at Pentecost. We must give our souls, minds, and hearts to God and say, "Change them!" We need to be changed in all that concerns the past, the present, and the future, to be gripped by Christ's painful death and by his resurrection.

It is because we are concerned with ourselves – because our hearts are full of self-love, envy, and other things – that we cannot respond as the people at Pentecost did. At that time the Spirit came and pierced their hearts like a sword cutting through bone and marrow. And so it must be our plea today: Give us thy Holy Spirit and pierce us. Have mercy on us, and change us to the depths of our being!

Heb. 4:12

If we want to tread in the footsteps of Jesus, we must recognize that there is an hour of God for everything, whether it is marriage, mission, persecution, or death itself. We may no longer determine our own timing for these things, for we have surrendered ourselves in such a way that God's hour is our own hour – whether of joy, sorrow, or drinking a bitter cup to the dregs with Jesus.

For those who are dearest to me, I wish nothing more than that they be ready to drink the bitter cup to the last. It is much easier for us than it was for Jesus, because he has gone before us in the way of suffering to the end. We must be set on fire with such love to him that we can drink the cup destined for us to the last drop with joy.

Jesus went the way of the cross for our sakes. But he suffered in vain if we are not willing to die for him, to lose ourselves for him. Let us ask God that our thoughts and feelings are moved by his death on the cross, his descent into hell, his resurrection, and his ascension into heaven.

You must find the humility of the cross. You can search the whole world, but you will find forgiveness of sins nowhere except at the cross.

Lk. 9:23–25

We cannot encounter Jesus without encountering the cross. His person emanates the way of suffering. Through his sacrifice his great love for all men floods our hearts and becomes in us an urge to go out to save those who are in the grip of darkness. If we love Jesus, the desire to suffer for him will well up quite naturally. I cannot imagine how one can follow Jesus without a deep understanding for his way of suffering.

We need to get past our personal struggles to experience the great thoughts of God. To experience personal salvation through the cross is important, but to remain at this stage is useless. The cross is so much greater than the personal; it embraces the whole earth and more than this earth.

There are secrets that only God knows. Christ's death on the cross is one such mystery. The Bible says that through the cross not only this earth but also heaven and all the powers and principalities belonging to the angel world will be reconciled to God. Man, and perhaps even the angels, cannot know the mysteries that lie behind all this. But one thing we know: Christ overcame death, the last enemy. And through the cross something took place which had power far beyond the limits of our earth, far greater than our souls can comprehend.

Col. 1:15–20

Salvation

Mt. 25:1–13 *From a letter:* In his parable of the ten virgins, Jesus emphasizes the reality of punishment for sin and the loss of eternal salvation. The thought of eternal punishment is certainly frightening. But John writes
1 Jn. 4:18 that complete love drives away fear, for fear still thinks of punishment, and he who thinks of punishment does not love fully. The tension between these two poles – the fear of punishment and the love that drives away all fear – can be overcome only by the experience of love.

If you love someone very deeply, you will not be afraid of him. In the same way, if you truly love Jesus, you will not fear him. You cannot serve Jesus out of fear.

2 Pt. 3:9 It is God's will that all men should be redeemed and that none should be lost. Yet the Gospels also say very clearly that none of us will be saved unless we experience rebirth through the Holy Spirit, unless we go through repentance and conversion and find faith. And Jesus, who has greater love than any man, speaks clearly of damnation. Even though God is almighty, and even though it is his express will that all be saved, he does
Acts 8:32 not force his will on us – his nature is that of the lamb,
Mt. 3:16 Christ, and the dove, the Holy Spirit. So it depends on us as individuals whether or not we open ourselves to

the grace of rebirth. First, however, we must become lowly and broken, for rebirth is not possible without sharp judgment. God's judgment is love.

Rom. 8

In Romans 8 Paul speaks about the salvation of the chosen or elect. One might ask, "What about the others? Will they also be saved?" Peter throws light on this question in his second letter, where he writes, "It is not that the Lord is slow in fulfilling his promise, as some suppose, but that he is very patient with you, because it is not his will for any to be lost, but for all to come to repentance." It is clear, then, that God wills that everyone, including his enemies, may repent and find salvation. But we should not become guilty of playing with his patience.

2 Pt. 3:9

When Christ is victorious in our hearts, it is not the result of a slow evolution – it does not mean becoming better and better. It means judgment and then change. Lukewarmness is not a choice. A person will either turn completely to Jesus or will ultimately be judged.

Rv. 3:16

The whole idea of the damnation of sinful man is very hard to accept and reconcile with the love of Jesus as he so powerfully revealed it on the cross at Golgotha. But anyone who remains bound by sin cannot enter the kingdom of God, otherwise the world would continue divided and evil. We do not

1 Cor. 6:9–11

understand the fullness of God's love. Yet we do know that Jesus carries the sins of the whole world, and that he stands before the throne of God. His sacrifice for the redemption of the world is the central point. We should never lose sight of that.

As a child I always had the feeling that someday the
masses–the working class–would be moved to come
nearer to God. Perhaps I was influenced by the many
anarchists, socialists, and religious socialists who stayed
at our house. But when I was older I read in the Book
of Revelation how one bowl of wrath after another
Rv. 16 would be poured over the earth, and still men would
not repent. This was very hard for me. I could not
accept the idea of only a very small fraction of humankind being saved. It went against my whole way of
thinking. I searched the Bible–the prophets and the
New Testament–with this one question in mind.

When I read the Gospel of John, I came across the
place where Jesus says that judgment will come over
the earth: "The prince of this world will be driven out,
Jn. 12:31–32 and I shall draw all men to myself." I do not know
how Jesus will do it, but I do believe that he will draw
all men to himself, and that he did not die on the
Mt. 7:13–14 cross for just a few people. Jesus says that the way to
truth is narrow and that few people will find it, that
most people walk the broad way that leads to damnation. This is undeniably true, but it would be terrible

if we were to think that we ourselves had found the narrow way, and if we had no love for those who go the broad way.

Jn. 8:1–11 The eighth chapter of John begins with the Pharisees
wanting to stone a woman caught in adultery, and it
Jn. 8:59 ends with their wanting to stone Jesus. Jesus angered
the Jews because he spoke frankly about who he was,
what his task was, and how he had come to save
humankind. The chapter raises a decisive question for
us and for every individual: Are we willing to believe
Jesus' words, or do we doubt them? Jesus says that if
Jn. 8:31–36 we do not believe, we are slaves; we are not free even
if we think we are free. He says that there is no other
way to find freedom, redemption, and liberation than
through faith in him.

Jn. 8:24 He also says, "If you do not believe, you will die
Jn. 8:51 in your sins," and "Those who obey me will never see
death." These words had to be said, for they are the truth, and they stand for all time. If we find faith, we will find freedom from sin, from the fear of death, and from the lovelessness of our time. But if we do not find faith, we will remain slaves to these things. The challenge to each of us is to love Jesus and accept the freedom he offers us.

Mt. 25:1–13 In the parable of the ten virgins Jesus is not speaking
of the world but of Christians. All those who went to

meet the Bridegroom were virgins; that is, they were all Christians. But five of them were wise and five foolish. They all had the outward form – the vessel. But they did not all have oil. The oil of which Jesus speaks is the Holy Spirit, the life that comes from God, and only five of them had that.

Mt. 5–7 In the Beatitudes we see the marks of those who have the Holy Spirit. They are poor in spirit, they mourn, they are meek, they hunger and thirst for righteousness, they are merciful and pure of heart, they are peacemakers, and they are persecuted for righteousness' sake. In fact, the whole Sermon on the Mount tells us how we should live: we should never come to prayer without forgiving our brother; we should love our enemies and bless those who curse us; we should not collect money or treasures on earth; we should put our whole trust in the Father; and we should use no force.

It is a sharp judgment that the foolish virgins are not allowed into the kingdom of heaven, and this is a two-fold call to us. The one is to watch and wait for the Holy Spirit so that he may change our soul and our being, and so that we may be reborn – so that we are touched daily by Jesus. The other is to live for those who are with us on the way to meet the bridegroom, and to call them to have oil in their lamps. The outer form is not enough; it is not enough to live in community or to follow the outer forms of Christianity even to the last. Discipleship must spring from a living heart.

It may be that God pre-ordains certain people to be his own. It is clear that John the Baptist was chosen before his birth, and I can also imagine that the Apostle Paul was meant to be what he was a long time before he was born. But if there is such a thing as certain people being ordained by God to be his, even before they are born, then how is it with all the rest? In the Old Testament we read, "'Have I any desire,' says the Lord God, 'for the death of a wicked man? Would I not rather that he should mend his ways and live?'" And in the New Testament we read, "It is not God's will for any soul to be lost, but for all to come to repentance." So the Bible makes it clear that God wants all men to be saved.

Lk. 1:15
Ez. 18:23
2 Pt. 3:9

Jesus said to Simon Peter, "Behold, Satan demands to have you, that he might sift you like wheat, but I have prayed for you that your faith may not fail; and when you have turned again, strengthen your brethren." I think Satan demands to sift us too, and we must ask Jesus to pray for us that our faith may not fail, also for the sake of our brothers.

Lk. 22:31–32

Whenever I fail, I keenly feel the words: "The Lord turned and looked." I am sure that Jesus has turned and looked at us many times – very sadly. When Jesus said that Peter would deny him, he was not just stating a predestined fact that left him untouched. It pained him even though he knew beforehand that it would

Lk. 22:61

happen. It was the same with Judas. When Jesus
Jn. 13:21 shuddered and said, "One of you will betray me," he suffered real agony. May we all have an open heart for the look Jesus gives us. He wants to protect his followers, but even after they are chosen by him they are still in danger of being lost.

Woe to us if we think we will get to heaven because we live in community. If we believe this, we don't love Christ enough.

Paul writes in his letter to the Romans that Jesus came not only for the Jews but for all men. He goes on to
Rom. 2:28 say, "The true Jew is not he who is such in externals; nor is the true circumcision the external mark in the flesh. The true Jew is he who is such inwardly." In the same way, the true Christian is not recognizable outwardly – even if he is baptized. To pour water over a person or immerse him in water is in itself no help toward salvation. "True circumcision is of the heart,
Rom. 2:29 directed not by written precepts but by the Spirit; such a man receives his commendation not from men but
Gal. 5:1, 6 from God." This is an important point: faith is not made up of written precepts. Paul was referring to the law of Moses, but today too, we can be enslaved by written laws – this is one of our dilemmas. We must

never give up the freedom of the Spirit, in which alone we can find peace in God.

Even if we do not completely understand the thoughts of Paul regarding salvation, the heart and the sense of his words are very easy to understand: the Pharisees kept the law but were still proud hypocrites, whereas "our argument is that a man is justified by faith, quite apart from his success in keeping the law." Rom. 3:28

The Holy Spirit

The Holy Spirit is like water, which seeks the lowest place. He comes only to the broken and humble heart.

After Jesus rose from the dead and ascended into heaven, the disciples waited in Jerusalem for the promised gift from heaven. Their expectation and waiting held them together day after day. And then the Holy Spirit came – both like a wind blowing and like fire burning. Everyone could hear the message of the glory of God in his mother tongue.

Acts 1:4

Acts 2:1–13

Then Peter challenged the crowd: "Jesus, whom *you* have crucified, is risen!" The people were cut to the heart and asked Peter, "What shall we do?" They were aware of their sinfulness. It is possible that some had cried, "Crucify him!" two months earlier. Peter said, "Change your life, and change your heart, and be baptized in the name of Jesus, and receive the forgiveness of sins."

Acts 2:22–41

Peter's offer was so startling that three thousand were gathered into the church! This great event of the pouring out of the Holy Spirit was the founding of the church, the first living, missionary church.

We all need this Holy Spirit. There are so many spirits at work today that are impure, destructive, rebellious, murderous, and unjust. We cannot unite in true community for one day without the gift of the Holy Spirit. Whether in our work, our worship, our singing, or our silence, we await this Spirit – the Spirit promised to us through the death of Jesus.

When the Spirit is poured out on a group of expectant people, something happens for the whole world. Therefore, when we pray for the Holy Spirit we should think beyond ourselves and ask God to break in over the whole, godless earth.

Mt. 3:16 When Jesus was baptized, the Holy Spirit descended upon him "like a dove." Kings have always had emblems, but they are usually something like a lion, an eagle, or a bear – something that sheds blood and is powerful. A dove is gentle. It harms no one. It flees from birds of prey. Through Adam's fall we are all birds of prey and drive the Holy Spirit away. If we resist the Spirit he withdraws. But if we are lowly and seek him, he will come to us. He comes without coercion or force and stays wherever he is accepted.

The experience of the Holy Spirit can never remain an individual experience: it will lead to community.
Acts 4:31–35 When the Spirit came over the disciples in Jerusalem, they became of one heart and one soul; they were so filled with love that they could no longer live for themselves. That is the greatest gift: to experience unity with Jesus Christ in community with others.

Jesus rejects all spiritual activity that is not proved by deeds of honest, brotherly love. He is uncompromising. He sharply opposes human, religious
Mt. 23:23–24 commandments that forget his main commandments of love, mercy, and compassion.

How can we live more fully by the Spirit? Let us take Mary, the mother of Jesus, as our example. Mary believed, she obeyed, the Spirit came upon her, and Jesus was born. The work of God began in her inmost heart. Like Mary, the church receives Jesus Christ through the Holy Spirit. When we obey Jesus – especially his words in the Sermon on the Mount and his farewell pleas to the disciples in the Gospel of John – the Spirit will come to us, and Christ will be born in our hearts anew.

We must accept the life and blood, spirit and soul of Jesus himself. It takes the life and the death of Jesus to free us from guilt because he was innocently executed. The pure life of Jesus – his soul filled with the Holy Spirit – streamed out from his body. His pure Spirit brought the kingdom. He is the source of the living Spirit who comes to the human spirit.

Lk. 23:46 The crucified one laid his spirit into the hands of his Father. From his Father he sent the Holy Spirit to the

church. He is commander and Lord over the church.
Rom. 14:7–8 In the Holy Spirit, Christ comes to us, and now we
1Jn. 4:16 no longer live for ourselves, but for him. Jesus Christ himself is among all who believe in him.

Jn. 13:34–35 Jesus told us to love one another. He does not mean that we love some people and are cold to others. He means that we are to love everyone. That is what happened at Pentecost. Those gripped by the Spirit were of one heart and one soul. All were included in this love. There were no cliques, no despising of one person and thinking highly of another. What happened at Pentecost was an experience of love, and the result was community. God is love.

From a letter: There is hardly anything more wonderful than Pentecost, when the Holy Spirit was poured out over Christ's disciples. The love among them was so great that they were of one heart and one soul, and they proclaimed the gospel, even though they knew they would have to suffer for it. Let us implore the Holy Spirit to fill our hearts too, with flames of fire, so that we may work in a suffering world for Christ's sake.

We all long for freedom in the depths of our being, freedom from anything that binds us to darkness,
2 Cor. 3:17–18 even to ourselves. God's Spirit is unbounded, free. When we respond to the heart and spirit of Jesus we have deep inner freedom, genuine relationships, and
Mt. 6:1–18 real understanding of others. Jesus opposes all outer show. Laws or commandments that don't stem from the depth of our hearts have a deadening effect. If we take commands literally, without the Spirit – the free Spirit – they are less than nothing. For what everyone hungers for is a relationship with the heart of God.

From a letter: Beloved brother and sister, I wish you the discovery that joy is life, and life should be joy. We only have to surrender to God's will and die to our own will to experience this. Then we'll understand the
Jn. 3:1 ff. words of Jesus to Nicodemus about rebirth and the coming of the Holy Spirit. We must pray for the gifts of the Holy Spirit: peace, faith, joy, and love.

1 Cor. 12–13 If we ask God for the gifts of the Spirit, let us be watchful about wanting to be honored by people. For ourselves we can ask for wisdom, a pure heart, more
Gal. 5:22–23 faith, hope, and love, more patience and compassion. But no one should ask for apostolic gifts or miraculous powers for himself. Instead, we should request these for the whole body of Christ. We all have to die with

Christ to such an extent that we are deaf to human praise. Please don't ever praise me. Jesus warned the Pharisees of this: "I do not accept praise from men…
Jn. 5:41, 44 How can you believe, when you receive glory from one another and do not seek the glory that comes from the only God?"

Jesus warns us about using religious words without deeds. We have to proclaim Jesus, but this does not
Mt. 7:15–23 mean we always have "Lord, Lord" on our lips. A good conscience responds with joy whenever someone speaks from the Holy Spirit. But when someone speaks from his own charisma or personality, and Jesus is pushed from the center, the Holy Spirit is hurt. We do not become holy after we are reborn. We remain sinful people who need the grace of forgiveness every day. This becomes very real when we encounter the seriousness of God's judgment.

Jn. 14:26 The Holy Spirit never witnesses to himself; he always witnesses to Jesus.

1 Cor. 2:1–5 To truly proclaim Christ means that he must live in
Mt. 26:75 you. Peter himself denied Jesus three times and wept bitterly for it. And he was not allowed to be the shep-
Jn. 21:15–17 herd of God's flock until he was asked three times if he loved Jesus. Peter could not work in God's vineyard

before that – before he had received the Spirit of the holy love of God.

After the resurrection Christ breathed on the apostles and said, "Receive the Holy Spirit." This same Spirit descended upon them again at Pentecost. These were shaking experiences which we dare not try to copy. I think people speak too lightly about being filled with the Spirit. In the early church, when the Holy Spirit was poured out, people repented. Where repentance isn't to be felt, be careful. If we have not honestly repented and believe in Jesus Christ, we have not received the Holy Spirit.

Jn. 20:22

The Spirit pierces hearts like a sword
 that cuts through bone and marrow.
We plead: give us your Holy Spirit
 and pierce us deep into the past,
 into the present, into the future.
May Jesus enter deep into our hearts and change them.
May he reach his hand into our past,
 to the ultimate beginning of our being.
The Holy Spirit can change all things.
We believe this.
For this, Jesus experienced godforsakenness
 on the cross.

As a consequence of Adam's fall, all of us battle against
Rom. 5:12 the terrible downward pull of sin – an inclination to pride and envy and all kinds of sin. Demons of evil thoughts and feelings defile us. Self-love and conceit mix with our good intentions. In all sharpness we must fight to purify ourselves from everything evil.

Jesus came to destroy the works of the devil. He also said these wonderful words, "When I drive out
Mt. 12:28 demons in the Holy Spirit, the kingdom of God has come to you." I have read this passage many times and have been comforted and enlivened by it. This promise can strengthen any soul that is tempted.

In all our struggles we should look to the cross. There, in prayer, any seeking soul can find victory. But going to the cross means death, too. In death, at the feet of Jesus on the cross, we find victory over any devil or demon. We can experience the kingdom of God now, in the Holy Spirit. We must die so that Christ radiates from us.

The Kingdom of God

It is quite clear that the kingdom of God cannot exist where bombs are being dropped on people, whether guilty or innocent, where there is racial hatred among men, where there is such poor distribution of food that some people starve while others have surplus food, or where people cannot find work because of automation.

If we really see the injustice of the world for what it is, we will long for the kingdom of God. Only when the hearts of men are moved toward love and peace will his righteousness break in. Those who remain unmoved, however, cannot take part in the kingdom.
Mt. 3:2 Therefore John the Baptist said, "Repent, for the
Mt. 6:33 kingdom of God is at hand." And Jesus said, "Seek
first the kingdom of God and his righteousness, and everything else will be yours as well."

Jesus came to prepare all men for the kingdom of God, which has not yet come, as we know only too well. He told us that the kingdom will be among us when we love God with our whole heart and soul, and when we love our neighbor as ourselves. If only we would do this, not just in words but in deed!

Jesus came not as a great king or president but as a humble baby. That is what people have not understood. He proclaimed the coming kingdom of God.

There has perhaps never been a time when this is more urgently needed than the present. Men have more power than ever, and the power of their weapons is frightening. The relationships of people, races, and nations, are unsolved, and those who have money rule.
Mt. 19:21 Jesus says we should become poor. If we obey him and give up worldly privileges and power over people, our hearts will be freed for the kingdom of God. Oh, if we could only glimpse what this kingdom means: repentance, glowing love, and God's rulership above everything!

Nations are building their freedom and security on the most dangerous weapons that have ever existed. Yet we are called to build our security on something else – that which is of God. And we long that something of God might be given to all nations. It is not enough to lead even the most perfect life of peace in church community. Our longing will be satisfied only when the whole earth comes under the rulership of God, not the rulership of force.

Jn. 6:11–15 When Jesus fed five thousand people with five loaves and two fishes, a remarkable thing happened: the people wanted to force him to become their king.
Jn. 6:26 ff. But Jesus said to them, "You come to me because I have fed you," and he rejected them. Then those who

wanted to make him king left him. Some of them were even hostile. After this Jesus said to the twelve, "All the others have gone away; do you want to leave me now too?" We must be ready to answer this question: Do we also want to leave?

It is significant that the people wanted to make Jesus king only after he gave them bread. This did not happen even when he raised someone from the dead. There is nothing wrong in itself with expecting God to give us bread, or expecting Jesus to fill our needs. Jesus taught us to ask our Father for our daily bread. But what he so sharply rejects is the building of a kingdom on that mammonistic level. He would rather lose his disciples than build his kingdom on a false foundation.

Jesus offers to give himself to each one of us to the extent that we become one flesh and one blood with him. This is not a philosophy, but real food; it is life. It changes everything in anyone who experiences it, not only for that moment but for all eternity.

Christ promises us eternal life in a kingdom based on faith, not on work and bread. Usually a king demands the blood of his subjects. But Christ gave his blood for his subjects. He gave his life and his body for the lives of others. At the time Christ offered his body to his disciples, he had – as far as we know – the largest following of his lifetime. But after this, many left him. That is why Jesus asked the twelve, "Do you
Jn. 6:67–68 also want to leave me?" Peter's answer is wonderful: "Lord, to whom shall we go? Your words are words of eternal life."

It is important for us to decide whether we want only a nice church with Jesus as its king, or the way of the cross. This must be very clear to us: Jesus' way is the way of the cross, of complete personal change, of a society on a completely different basis than work and bread and privileges. We must be willing to be surrounded by enemies and to be despised for going his way.

The way society has developed in this century of such tremendous injustice and bloodshed shows us that salvation and redemption cannot come from men; they must come from God. All the more we must call on God to reveal once again his kingdom of righteousness and justice among men.

Jesus is the kingdom of God. When he forgave sins, that was the kingdom of God. When he gathered his friends in unity, that was the kingdom of God. When
Mt. 12:28 he drove out demons and impure spirits, that was the kingdom of God. Every deed of his mission among men was the kingdom of God.

I sometimes wonder whether our community has not completely forgotten the kingdom of God, and whether the distinction between personal salvation and the kingdom is clear enough to us. Both are of great importance. Eternal salvation is very important–it is wonderful to experience the nearness of Christ and to be redeemed by him. But the kingdom of God is still greater!

The nearness of the kingdom of God cannot be
Mt. 4:17 measured in terms of time. Jesus said "The kingdom of heaven is at hand!" And paradoxical as it sounds, it was nearer at that time than it is now. It was not nearer in terms of time, but in terms of space.

Jas. 5:16 The kingdom of God must be fought for and wrestled
Mk. 9:29 for. The prayers of men and women have tremendous influence in this fight.

If we love Christ and his cause, we will have the interest of his kingdom at heart. Christ came to this earth and suffered in order to bring the kingdom on earth, and his church is entrusted with the very great task of mission for this kingdom.

What a mighty thing it is to live for God's kingdom! Do not shrink back. Live for it; look for it, and you will find that it is so powerful it will completely overwhelm you–it will solve every problem on earth. Everything will be new, and each person will love the other in Christ. All separation brought about by death will be overcome, and love will rule.

The commission we are given by Jesus as a church is to work for his kingdom and his future reign. There is nothing greater on earth than to work for this. Let us live intensely and use our time for the kingdom! Let us love one another!

God needs a place on earth where he can break in. Such a place was there in Mary, whose willingness made it possible for Christ to be born in Bethlehem. If God can enter in even one place, whether in Bethlehem, China, Russia, Vietnam – in a human heart anywhere – it is like the opening of a door. If the door to a room is opened even a little, light can come in. And if God's light enters and moves the hearts of just two or three people on earth, it will affect all the rest. It will even affect presidents, prime ministers, generals, and soldiers. I cannot believe that humans are so isolated from one another that it has no effect.

Rom. 5:12–21 Just as through Adam the whole of humankind fell, so through Jesus – the "second Adam," the true man, and God himself – the whole of humankind can find freedom, healing, and redemption.

Let us call upon God and ask him that we may fight for his kingdom. The more deeply we enter this fight, the more deeply we will experience the cross of Christ, the resurrection, and Pentecost – and the nearer the kingdom will be to us. Live intensively in the expectation of the Lord! He who does not wait for the Lord in every aspect of his life does not wait at all. I ask myself every evening, have I really loved enough, hoped enough, fought enough, worked enough? The expectation of the kingdom must lead to deeds.

Karl Barth* once said that the kingdom of God must be revealed to us as something completely different from us, something completely independent from us which we cannot mix with our own selves. This is, I think, a very important recognition. Unless we die to ourselves for his sake, we remain in opposition to him and unworthy of him.

God could have closed human history at Golgotha, when Jesus overcame the devil and death. But he did not do that, and evil had a further chance. This is a mystery to us. Many people from all nations are won for the kingdom of God, but many others are misled. I do not dare to guess why this is so, but I know that God is the ruler of the universe and that his judgment must stand. We read that those who are misled, those
Rv. 14:9–10
who "worship the beast and its image," will receive its mark on their forehead or hand and will drink the wine of God's wrath. We don't know when this will

*Karl Barth, Swiss theologian, 1886–1968.

happen, or when the breaking in of God's kingdom will come, but we must raise our children so that they are ready to stand firm when it does. Our children must be courageous enough to stand for the truth.

How does the kingdom of God relate to the last judgment? How will the kingdom come, and what will it be like? Much is shown us through the sayings of Jesus himself, through the writings of the early church, and through the working of the Spirit in the individual heart. Yet Jesus said that the hour of the coming kingdom was known to the Father alone and that even he, the Son of God, did not know when it would come. We can approach these questions only with greatest awe, reverence, and caution. At the same time, though, we see how very concerned the early Christians were with the coming of the kingdom. All the words of the apostles point to it.

Mt. 24:36

We do not know how near or far we are from the kingdom of God in terms of time. But we know we can be very near or very far from it in spirit, and that is the decisive question. Jesus said that we can expect signs of the coming kingdom, and some of these signs are evident today. Yet he also said that the last day would come like a thief in the night; that is, at a moment when no one expects it or is thinking about it.

Lk. 21:9–11

Lk. 12:39–40

There are many mysteries we cannot solve because God wishes to keep them hidden. But we can rejoice in this: the coming of the kingdom is certain, and it is a kingdom of peace, victory, and justice.

We do not know why God allowed death and evil to enter creation, yet we do know that man let himself be seduced by evil. In the same way, we do not know what struggle God carried on against evil before the creation of man, or the proportion and nature of man's task in this struggle, but we do know that it was a decisive struggle and that it brought the Son of God himself to the cross.

Rv. 19:11–21

In the Revelation of John we read of a battle that will take place in heaven at the end time. The church – as the Body of Christ – has to carry on the same battle here upon earth. Just as God did not spare the suffering of his own Son but delivered him up to suffer the greatest need, so too, at the expense and sacrifice of the church, the kingdom will break in.

The separation of the spiritual from the material, of the soul from the body, is death, but unity is life. Jesus brought the message of a new kingdom where soul and body, spiritual and material, will no longer be separated. In this new kingdom the Creator will be one with his creation.

When we look at the earth as it is now, we see that judgment is inevitable. In fact, the sin of men is already carrying out this judgment. Yet if we deeply consider the words of Christ, we will find that grace, mercy, and compassion will triumph over judgment.

We expect a new heaven and a new earth, but we must not trouble ourselves with exactly how and when the kingdom will come. We know only that
2 Pt. 3:12 it is coming. And since Peter says that the church must expect, help, and hasten on the coming of God, we know it is our task to see that something of his kingdom is revealed and made living among us.

In the beginning, even before the creation of the universe, was the endlessly loving Father, God, and with him the Word, which is Jesus Christ, and the Holy Spirit. At the end of time, too, God alone will rule. Groaning creation will be redeemed and the
Rv. 7:17 universe will be joyful. There will be pure joy, love,
Rv. 21:4 harmony, and justice. God will wipe away every tear, and there will be no death, sorrow, or pain. The longing for this time burns in the heart of every being, spiritual or human.

You may wonder about the millennium, the resurrection of the just, and the future of God's kingdom. Simply leave it all to God. We face many mysteries regarding the future; we do not know the reason for

this, that, or the other. The main thing is that in the
1 Cor. 15:28 end God is all in all. He will triumph over all evil
and over all that is hostile to him. That should be our
greatest expectation.

What a great gift it would be if we could see a little of the great vision of Jesus – if we could see beyond our small lives! Certainly our view is very limited. But we can at least ask him to call us out of our small worlds and our self-centeredness, and we can at least ask to feel the challenge of the great harvest that must be gathered – the harvest of all nations and all people, including the generations of the future.

Index of Bible References

Other Titles from Plough

Freedom from Sinful Thoughts by J. Heinrich Arnold. Pastoral advice on finding freedom and wholeness in a world full of distractions and temptations.

Homage to a Broken Man: The Life of J. Heinrich Arnold by Peter Mommsen. This biography tells of the crucibles that made Arnold the man he was and gave his thoughts their depth.

God's Revolution by Eberhard Arnold. This selection of writings by a man who left the established church in order to live out the gospel calls the reader to a completely different way.

Why We Live in Community by Eberhard Arnold, with two interpretive talks by Thomas Merton. Inspirational thoughts on the basis, meaning, and purpose of community.

Why Forgive? by Johann Christoph Arnold. Stories from people who have earned the right to talk about forgiving, and about the peace of mind they have found in doing so.

Following the Call: Living the Sermon on the Mount Together edited by Charles E. Moore. Fifty-two readings to spark weekly group discussion on putting Jesus' most central teachings into practice.

Called to Community: The Life Jesus Wants for His People edited by Charles E. Moore. Fifty-two readings on living in intentional Christian community.

Plough Publishing House
www.plough.com
1-800-521-8011 • 845-572-3455

PO Box 398 • Walden, NY 12586 • USA
Brightling Rd • Robertsbridge • East Sussex TN32 5DR • UK
4188 Gwydir Highway • Elsmore, NSW 2360 • Australia